D1639136

ARGYLL CURIOSITIES

ARGYLL CURIOSITIES

Marian Pallister

BIRLINN

First published in 2007 by
Birlinn Limited
West Newington House
10 Newington Road
Edinburgh
EH9 1QS

www.birlinn.co.uk

ISBN13: 978 1 84158 531 4
ISBN10: 1 84158 531 9

British Library Cataloguing-in-Publication Data
A catalogue record for this book is available from
the British Library

Typeset by Mercat Press in Adobe Garamond

Printed and bound by Cromwell Press, Trowbridge

To Ken

CONTENTS

ACKNOWLEDGEMENTS

I am hugely indebted to former archivist for Argyll and Bute, Murdo MacDonald, and to Jackie Davenport and Marina Campbell in the Lochgilphead archives office for all their help.

I would also like to thank Dr Crinan Alexander of the Royal Botanic Garden, Edinburgh; Dr Derek Alexander of the National Trust for Scotland; Argyll and Bute library staff at Campbeltown and Oban; Alison Arden of the *Oban Times*; Brian Balmain, Chairman of Bute Victorian Company; Belfast Public Libraries; Maureen Bell for access to her collection of photographs; Jenny Campbell; Dun Laoghaire library staff; the Glens of Antrim Historical Society; John Haddington; Aidan Hart for kind permission to use his icon of St Columba from his website: www.aidanharticons.com; Rob Hunter for his photographic contribution; the MacKenzie Collection, Scottish Slate Islands Heritage Trust; Euan McLaughlin, Island of Luing; Ian Marshall; Sarah Moore of the Hebridean Trust; the National Library of Scotland; the Newcomen Society; the library of the North of England Institute of Mining and Mechanical Engineers; Professor Roland A. Paxton, School of the Built Environment, Heriot-Watt University; Derek Prescott of Lochgoilhead for access to documents; the Society of Antiquaries of Scotland for supplying illustrations and information; Tackle and Books, Tobermory; Ronald Tognieri of Campbeltown; Ivan Young and the Grampian Speleological Society for information and photographs; Jack Murray of Michigan, USA, for kind permission to access his family website; the late Duncan McArthur of Peninver; and Muriel and Jim Adam, Edinburgh.

INTRODUCTION

When Martin Martin set off at the turn of the eighteenth century on his journeyings to discover the 'Curiosities of Art and Nature' in the Western Isles of Scotland, many people were already travelling abroad on the Grand Tour. Indeed, Martin himself had gone to university in Leiden after studying for an MA at Edinburgh in 1681, and he was no stranger to the sights of Europe.

Even then, despite decades of dispute in Britain and sporadic wars in Europe, there were many accounts being written about France, Italy and Switzerland; but when Martin undertook to put the Western Isles under the microscope, his was the first book about this part of Scotland. In the preface to his 1703 publication he chided those who saw nothing of worth on their own doorstep and instead travelled to more exotic locations.

'The Modern Itch after Knowledge of Foreign Places is so prevalent,' he wrote, 'that the generality of Mankind bestow little thought or time upon the Place of their Nativity; it is become Customary for those of Quality to Travel young into Foreign Countries, whilst they are absolutely strangers at home; and many of them when they return, are only loaded with the superficial Knowledge, as the bare Names of Famous Libraries, Stately Edifices, Fine Statues, Curious Paintings, late Fashions, new Dishes, new Tunes, new Dances, Painted Beauties and the like.'

And yet, as he discovered, the Western Isles were a cornucopia of curiosities, and the accounts which he gave of them were not simply of interest to 'those of Quality' who had the time and the ability to read for their own edification, but were of great value to the community of which he wrote. Almost two centuries later, when members of the Napier Commission read his account of the Western Isles in their investigations into the conditions of Scotland's crofters, they found it most helpful. Martin explained the working relationship between crofters and traditional lairds, most of whom had long since disappeared, leaving the land in the custody of many who sought only profit and eschewed moral responsibility.

The world has changed almost beyond recognition since Martin Martin undertook his journey, and indeed since the Napier Commission deliberated on the state of the late Victorian crofter more than a century ago. And yet, human nature remains the same. We are still more inclined to go off to foreign places than to study our native lands. A cheap flight to Prague, a weekend in New York, or a holiday *gîte* in the Dordogne bring knowledge of interesting architecture, curious paintings or new recipes – or just a chance to indulge in 'new tunes, new dances, painted beauties, and the like' – but often at the expense of discovering the fascinating curiosities which lie on our doorsteps.

Only parts of Argyll came under Martin Martin's scrutiny and the intrepid travellers who followed in his footsteps – Johnson and Boswell, Thomas Pennant, Lord Teignmouth and Lord Cockburn among them – did not always look into situations but rather at them. Martin Martin asked the 'why' and 'how' questions, while tourists like Johnson were more inclined to complain about the beds, and Lord Teignmouth had a touch of 'let them eat cake' in his attitude. Visiting Colonsay in the late eighteenth century the latter scratched his head in disbelief that despite a grant of between £10 and £12 from the laird to build chimneyed fireplaces, people still insisted on setting their fire in the middle of the floor so that the children – and chickens and calves – could coorie round it.

Argyll – both its islands and its mainland, stretching from the frontiers of Lochaber to the tip of Kintyre – was and remains a county of curiosities. Curious people, curious situations, curious circumstances; curious customs, buildings, beliefs and botany.

There has never been an era in which curiosities in this western extremity of Scotland have not been turned up. Its very geology is singular, and the expert can place to within yards where a pebble or a boulder originated. Argyll's shape is like no other in these islands; its peninsulas and mountain ranges marked out territories for the people who found their way here nine thousand years ago. Its caves provided vast shelters as big as any mansion built in the nineteenth century, and archaeological studies of those around Oban have proved vital in the study of Mesolithic incomers to Argyll.

We should perhaps not be overcritical of the Church of Scotland minister who in the 1792 *Statistical Account* of Kilmartin wrote that there was nothing of interest in the glen in which his church sat. This glen is now on the international archaeological map as a highly important site, but who can blame a man who daily tripped over standing stones, cists, cairns and the rock art of a previous civilisation for not seeing the wood for the trees? Curiosities are what daily life is made of in Argyll. I walk a hundred yards from my back door and see sheep seeking out the warmth of the sun on boulders carved with millennia-old cup-and-ring marks. I cross the road to a churchyard where medieval grave slabs are so abundant that they are almost an embarrassment. There are wild orchids, some extremely rare, in nearby meadows. As a community, we objected to plans for an industrial installation because its proposed site is the home of rare dragonflies and martins. Goldfinches fight with bullfinches at my bird feeder. This is the norm, so where do we look for curiosity value?

There are many who have had curious ideas about changing the face of Argyll; why did someone want a motorway to Glasgow; a 3-mile-long runway across Crinan Moss, an important wetland site that harbours rare insects; and a nuclear power station at Crinan Harbour? There are many who have sought to enhance Argyll with curious architectural, educational and industrial plans; Argyll has often resisted even when the authorities said, 'yes'. There are many who have used its geography and speleology under curious circumstances to try to achieve their own ends – and many curious circumstances have conspired to change the course of history.

The aggression of the Norsemen, the fractiousness of the medieval clan leaders, the factionalism of the British Civil Wars of the seventeenth century; the fervour of the Pretenders' uprisings and the subsequent repressions all provided curious situations for curious deeds. In the calm and, for some, prosperity of the late eighteenth and the nineteenth century, engineers, architects and philanthropic men of genius and vision had their own curious take on how Argyll should be shaped. But Argyll has always had a mind of its own: its mountains, mists and seas – or the supernatural beings who inhabit them – have always had a curious knack of making sure that man does not get too high an opinion of himself or think that he can impose on the spirit and landscape of this ancient land.

There are many obvious curiosities in Argyll, and I hope that people will not be too disappointed to find that these have not been my choices. In looking beyond the obvious, I found Argyll all too generous in offering situations, plans, people and events which, in the words of Alice, got 'curiouser and curiouser'. I hope that I have asked the same 'how' and 'why' questions which Martin Martin posed as he made his journey around the Western Isles, and that the answers – given generously by the documents of the past and the people of the present – put Argyll's curiosities into a context which invites readers to explore further, and not simply to go off looking for fine statues, stately edifices and painted beauties elsewhere.

1

STONE

A few miles south of Inveraray the A83 drops down to the shore of Loch Fyne before climbing again through the village of Lochgair. On the shore side, at the tricky corner which takes travellers into the village, a white wall stands either side of an iron gate. On the left of the gate a sign announces that this is the Loch Gair Scottish Hydro Electricity project. Water tumbles down to this station from Loch Glashan, a man-made loch high in the hills west of the road. On the right side of the gate the white wall is curiously punctuated by an asymmetrical arch, and a plaque is also set into the wall's whitewashed rendering. The bend in the road, marked by a plethora of speed-restriction signs, is severe enough and sudden enough to prevent most modern travellers from stopping to read the plaque and trace the curve of the dark stone arch. And so the arch remains little more than an eyebrow raised at distracted motorists.

The Glashan arch at Loch Gair Power Station.

Yet this ancient stone may hold the secret of one of Mid Argyll's most curious building projects – a project which tradition says invoked the Temple of Jerusalem and the Devil. Written records introduce a drowned settlement and a garrulous young builder's mate into the equation. The stone itself is evidence of a time when the Earth was young and in a state of upheaval. The Mid Argyll and Cowal volume of the *Royal Commission on the Ancient and Historical Monuments of Scotland* describes the geology of the area as a variety of sandstones, shales and limestone 'metamorphosed by the mountain-building movements of the Caledonian period' into quarzites, schists and phyllites, and marbles. In subsequent ages, there were igneous intrusions into this mix. Quartz-porphyry sills of the Lower Red Sandstone period (495–440 million years ago) are present towards the northern end of Loch Fyne at Furnace and Crarae, where they have been extensively quarried over the millennia. The quarry at Furnace, to the north of Lochgair, is now the only known source of porphyry in Scotland and its stone has a variable grey or pink colour because of the iron oxide minerals it contains.

In the nineteenth century Furnace and Crarae were major suppliers of paving stone for Glasgow, but the stone found on Loch Fyne's shores has had many uses throughout the millennia. Once man had begun to lay his footprints in Mid Argyll, this western shore of Loch Fyne provided stone for many different needs. Some four thousand years before the birth of Christ the early inhabitants who settled around what we know today as Crarae and Lochgair were already farming, and while their agricultural methods may have been simple, their culture was complex. They quarried the local stone to create elaborate burial cairns, and by about 1400 BC, on the shore at the area which became Brainport, a sophisticated observatory was designed using slabs of rock to plot out the position of the sun at the summer solstice. Derek Alexander, archaeologist for the National Trust for Scotland, which now owns Crarae Gardens, has reported the remains of a Neolithic chambered cairn in the lower garden, a Bronze Age cairn nearby, and a medieval burial ground marked by stone monuments.

From the early sixth century AD onwards, Christian missionary monks came over from Ireland and their followers hewed stone from the Loch Fyne quarries to build chapels and monasteries. A chapel site and burial ground lie some 40 metres from the older chambered cairn. This was Killevin chapel, perhaps named for St Éibhinn, a woman associated with the Celtic St Bride. A massive cross shaft from the eighth or ninth century has been found on the site of Killevin in the confines of today's Crarae Gardens, but the masons who for generations dressed the stone quarried on the shores of Loch Fyne also seem to have been responsible for work far beyond the area of their local quarries. The medieval chapel at Kilmory on the seaboard of the Craignish peninsula to the north-west of Crarae, for example, bears evidence of stone taken from the Fyneside quarries. There is also growing evidence that the quarrymen's skills were commissioned by the ruling family on Loch Aweside when a church was planned above Fincharn Castle.

Fincharn Castle itself has a role to play in this curious tale, because, like all castles, it was owned by people of wide-reaching power and influence. Loch Awe and Loch Fyne were both formed by glaciers, which left behind them convenient routes of travel. Loch Awe runs from west to east and Loch Fyne from north to south, and from prehistoric times each provided easy passage in rough country. Several passes across the hills between them linked the two important waterways. Where there are such super-highways, people have always used them for both legitimate and illegitimate purposes. Some will settle along the edges and some will try to control them. In the case of Loch Awe and Loch Fyne, the traffic comprised cattle and monks, princes and brigands. Monks and hermits from the earliest Christian times came here and Columba himself was active in the area: just a few miles to the west of both lochs is Dunadd fort, where in AD 574 the Celtic saint anointed the first Christian king in the isles of Britain. As the next millennium dawned, the power in Scotland had moved east, but there were still important families controlling Mid Argyll – an area then known as Glassary. In what is considered to be the oldest existing charter of property in Argyll, King Alexander II granted Fyncharne and substantial lands to Gillascop MacGilchrist in 1240.

The Fyncharne property – later known as Fionncharn and then Fincharn – was then held by Master Ralph of Dundee and descendants of John and Gilbert of Glassary. In 1346 it was united with the former property of Ewen, Gillascop MacGilchrist's brother, making a powerful estate known as the barony or lordship of Glassary. Sometimes referred to as Castle of Glassary, Fyncharne's lands were regranted to Gilbert of Glassary by a royal charter of 1374. This allowed Gilbert's daughter to succeed to the property. As she had married Alexander Scrymgeour, the hereditary constable of Dundee and standard-bearer of Scotland, these

Argyll lands were now in the hands of one of the most powerful families in Scotland – and would remain so until 1668. During the tenure of this powerful family, buildings were commissioned to reflect their position in the area. Churches were erected at Craignish, Killevin and Kilneuair, which marked the boundaries of the large parish over which the Scrymgeours held sway, and they were all similar in their stylish design.

The word Kilneuair (Cill an Iubhair) means 'chapel of the yew trees', an echo of the fusion which saw Christianity sympathetically embrace the native Argyll worship of nature. Although the name was first recorded in 1394, a chapel had probably been established on this site overlooking Loch Awe and the strategic position of Fincharn Castle several centuries before the decision to build a grander church was taken in the late 1200s. The early chapel was probably the Columban site known as Cella Diuni. This new church at the south-west end of Loch Awe was, however, to be the seat of ecclesiastical power in the area of Glassary, just as Fincharn Castle was the seat of secular power.

Kilneuair was in a strategic position, standing at the start of one of the two main hill routes between Loch Awe and Loch Fyne, and by the time of the royal charter Kilneuair was a developing settlement. In the course of the centuries following the 1240 charter, a great cattle market called A'margadh Dhu – the 'black' (Dhu) presumably referring to the colour of the cattle rather than the more modern connotation of 'black market' – developed there as its hill route became the favoured drove road for traffic coming from Islay and Jura en route to the Lowlands via Auchindrain. Despite this, when the Kilneuair church was proposed, there may have been some surprise and even dissension at its usurpation of the status of the earlier church at Killevin. Perhaps still greater surprise and dissension were expressed when, as the *New Statistical Account* of 1844 recalls, it was decided that this new church should be built in the manner of the Temple of Jerusalem, 'without a hammer being laid on a stone at the site of it'.

Solomon, the man who realised the plans for the Temple of Jerusalem, employed 80,000 stonecutters in hills at sufficient distance from Jerusalem that the noise of their hammers wouldn't be heard at the site of the holy building. The stone was transported by 70,000 carriers from the quarries to the temple, and 3,300 foremen supervised the operation, according to the First Book of Kings, Chapter V. In the following chapter, the Bible tells us that 'only finished stones cut at the quarry were used, so that no hammer or axe or any iron tool was heard in the House while it was being built'. The stones were ready to be put in place when they arrived on site. According to the Rev. Colin Smith of Inveraray, who drew up a history of the area for the Rev. Dugald Campbell of Glassary to include in the *New Statistical Account* of 1844, the stone for the medieval church at Kilneuair was found and dressed 'at a quarry close to Killevin on Fyneside'. Tradition, Mr Campbell submitted, held that 'on a particular day duly appointed, people attended in such numbers as to form one close rank from Killevin to Kil-neuair, a distance of twelve miles, and that each stone, as raised at the quarry or hewing station, was handed from one man to another along the whole rank until it was fixed by the last of them in its place at the building'.

While kings David and Solomon may have had the power to employ tens of thousands to carry out the holy project of raising the huge temple which was eventually consecrated at Jerusalem in 953 BC, the idea of a human chain being formed across the hills between Loch Fyne and Loch Awe to transport every stone of a new chapel is somewhat more curious. Could the medieval rulers of the lands of Kilmichael have persuaded so many men to hand boulder after boulder across this rough Argyll terrain? Was it a day in July with midges driving them mad? Was it a day in October, with soft rain from the Atlantic seeping through their clothes? Or did the gales sweep across the Leacann Moor while the stones tore at the men's hands until they bled? The Temple of Jerusalem – admittedly built on a much grander scale – took seven years to complete; tradition claims that the stones were carried from Killevin to Kilneuair in a day.

Large portions of the walls of the church which is said to have resulted from that curious day's work are now crumbling and overgrown. Yew trees may have given Kilneuair its name, but a mongrel tangle of trees and bushes has pushed up into its nave, while plantations of conifers have swamped the site of the Black Market and parts of the track over the hills along which the men are said to have heaved the cut stones. Kilneuair is now an elegant little ruin hiding in the trees above Loch Awe; the crumbling Fincharn Castle below it a reminder of the power that once emanated from this remote western fringe.

Despite two subsequent periods of construction, there is still evidence of that first bold building. The chancel and the eastern half of the north wall date from the thirteenth century and are built of well-coursed rubble masonry which incorporates rounded boulders – was it these which

Kilneuair's medieval epidiorite font.

were carried over the hills? The west half of the north wall is late medieval and there is a medieval epidiorite font which was re-erected in the building in 1916 and maintains a brave battle against the undergrowth. The south wall was rebuilt in the sixteenth century using thin slabs of local schist. In this part there are sandstone dressings and some of moulded epidiorite.

Also known as the Church of Columba in Glassary, the little ruin is surrounded by the grave slabs of the great and the good of the area – and of those whose names have become legend because of the essential roles they played in the everyday life of Loch Aweside. Three medieval tapered grave slabs decorated with armed figures, dragonheads, plants and a Latin cross ought to be rescued from encroaching nature. A slab bearing the MacPhedran name – the family who ferried people across Loch Awe from the 1300s and paid 10 shillings, barley, oats, cheese and a sheep to the Campbell family for the privilege of holding the charter to ferry – is one of the few still legible in the churchyard. To the west of the church is a pretty little fairy-tale building with narrow pointed windows. This burial enclosure is not, however, the medieval edifice it appears to be: it belongs to the late eighteenth century.

By the sixteenth century, when the south wall was being repaired, power in the area was shifting. The Campbells, who had granted a charter to the MacPhedrans, were steadily taking over the land, and Kilmichael Glassary had replaced Kilneuair as the most important church in the sprawling parish by 1563. Even so, the *New Statistical Account* says that the church remained a place of veneration long after it ceased to be a place of worship. Local people were convinced that the walls were haunted either by the spirits of saints or of the dead who were 'unemancipated from purgatory'. Even Auld Nick is said to have lurked around the church. The story related by the Rev. Dugald Campbell in the *New Statistical Account* says that a local tailor, who was something of a betting man, was so sure that the spirits were nothing more than superstitious nonsense that he offered to sit in the church at midnight and sew a pair of trews. He had no sooner sat cross-legged to start stitching by the light of his torch than a sepulchral voice called out and he saw a huge hand coming out of the graves. The voice spoke in the tailor's own tongue – the Gaelic – and said, '*Am faic thu a chrog mhor liath so a thailleir?*' ('Seest thou this huge hoary hand, tailor?') The tailor bravely replied that he could see the hand but he would carry on sewing. The voice demanded, '*Am faic thu an ceann mor liath so a thailleir?*' ('Seest thou this large grey head, tailor?') Back came the tailor's response that he could see the head but would carry on sewing. The Devil – for that is who the *New Statistical Account* records was addressing the tailor – continued to make different parts of his skeleton appear. When the bony frame was complete, the tailor decided it was time to go. As he fled, according to Dugald Campbell, 'the bony hand that was stretched out to seize him struck, and left its impression on the wall'. Although the mark is impossible to see in the twenty-first century without imagination and goodwill towards the legend, there are those who until recent times have claimed to trace on the sandstone block on the inside of the eastern jamb of the nave door a five-toed print known as the Devil's Hand.

Such curious legends surrounding one small, ancient building. How could the stones for an entire church have been transported across 12 such hostile miles? Why should the Devil choose to haunt such a remote building or the spirits of the dead remain in the church's stones? Loch Awe had its own sources of boulder and there could have been no need for rubble masonry to be passed from hand to hand across a wild moor. And yet, the curious nature of the Fyneside stone, its like found

The wooden-scaffolded exterior wall of Kilneuair Chapel, a ruin
which holds many legends.

nowhere else in Scotland according to one geologist, has continued to
exert its power down the ages. Some six hundred years after the construction of the Kilneuair church, the good citizens of Glasgow were so
impressed by the stone to be found on Loch Fyneside that they had it
transported by boat to enhance their roads as the city grew in stature and
wealth. They did not, however, know the local legends which imbued
the stone with supernatural powers. And they certainly could not have
forseen that when their burgers took that a day-trip to Crarae quarry
on 26 September 1886 to witness the stones' excavation, it would end
in tragedy.

This strange twist in the curious tale of the Loch Fyne stones is almost
as bizarre as that of the tailor, the trews and Auld Nick, but this time
there were witnesses and the whole sorry business was recorded not only
in the Scottish newspapers but throughout the British press. At that
time, Crarae Quarry – surely not the same one from which the Kilneuair
stones were said to have come – was leased by Messrs William Sim and
Faill, paving stone contractors. The paving stones they produced were
being acquired by the Police and Statute Labour Committee of Glasgow
Town Council, and to celebrate fifty years of the committee's existence, an

outing to the quarry was planned. Members of the committee, councillors and other dignitaries sailed on the steamer *Lord of the Isles*. The steamer did a daily trip from Greenock to Inveraray and on this occasion was commandeered by the council so that they could view what was termed a 'monster blast' at the Crarae quarry.

The headline in the *Oban Times* of Saturday 2 October, reads:

FRIGHTFUL DISASTER AT LOCHFYNE

Beneath it, readers were told that on the previous Saturday seven people were 'thrown into eternity' and '60 temporarily overcome by the issue of sulphurous gas from the chinks and boulders of 80,000 tons of granite which had been exploded a short time before by nearly seven tons of gunpowder'.

This 'monster blast' was not laid on especially for the entertainment of Glasgow Town Council. For a number of years the proprietors had successfully organised summer explosions at Crarae and at Furnace, and

Crarae quarry, where a monster blast brought disastrous results.

they had been found to be a good way of getting the rock for the pavements of Glasgow and other cities. These blasts were obviously something of a spectacle and were considered to be such a good day out that they filled the *Lord of the Isles* every time a blast was advertised. In fact, there had been such a blast as recently as 7 July. On this particular sunny Saturday, one of the last holidays of the season according to the *Oban Times*, nearly two hundred people joined the steamer at Princes Pier in Greenock and many more went on board at the stops along the way. The crowds were entertained by the steamer's orchestra until, at Crarae, a bell was rung and the steamer stopped at the jetty there. The newspaper reported that 'All was silent, all were, with bated breath, eagerly watching the painted disc or large bull's eye upon the quarry face, for that point of the rock was the place to be exploded. Three whistles from the steamer's horn was the signal for the men to fire the mine.'

The result was spectacular. The noise of the explosion echoed around the hills, the dust rose and rocks began to tumble into the bowl of the quarry. At this point, around a hundred passengers disembarked and the steamer then left to take the rest of the passengers on to Inveraray. Of the party which rushed forward to see the rock fall, many were members of Glasgow Town Council, but there were also reporters from newspapers all around the British Isles and a number of women and children. The quarryman shouted 'Hello there! Don't go near the quarry – sulphurous gas!', but the *Oban Times* reported that no one heeded the warning. Was it given in Gaelic, the language of Mid Argyll of the day? Or was it given in a strange English accent? Many quarry workers were itinerant and their dialects could have been difficult to understand. Or was it simply that this was too good a show to miss and the crowd therefore suffered from selective deafness? Whatever made them ignore the warning, soon people were suffering from much worse. Cries of 'Help! Help! I'm choking' came from the quarry. Over forty people collapsed, first onto their hands and knees and then rolling over 'like dead persons onto rough broken crags'. Of course, the people left outside the quarry then rushed in to help and they, too, were overcome.

There was sulphurous hydrogen oozing out in volumes, according to the *Oban Times* reporter. For most, the effects did not last long, and forty people regained consciousness and were dragged to the beach. For seven people the fumes were too powerful and they died either at the quarry or later in hospital.

Those who lost their lives were Councillor Thomas Duncan, who had a letterpress business in Sauchiehall Street, Glasgow; Mr Matthew Waddell, the proprietor of one of Glasgow's largest restaurants, at 60 Union Street; Mr James Shaw, son of Bailie Shaw, a Glasgow accountant; Mr Peter Stevenson, of Forest Road, Glasgow, who was an optician in Edinburgh; Mr Steel, a well-known electro-plater from Belfast; Mr John Small, an elderly blacksmith from Ayrshire; and Bailie John Young of St Vincent Crescent, Glasgow, who had been a member of the council for twenty years and had been invited to witness the blast with the Statute Labour Committee. It was not simply a day out for Bailie Young: he had been charged as a representative of his fellow citizens with 'examining the granite stones which were to be placed on the Glasgow streets'. Although he survived the journey back to Greenock, he died the following morning in Greenock Infirmary.

The journalists who joined the *Lord of the Isles* found themselves part of the main story of the day. Some, like Mr Harvey of *The Scotsman* and Mr Temple, chief reporter of the *Glasgow Mail*, were overcome by the fumes. Mr Temple fell into a pool of stagnant water and was only saved 'with difficulty' by Councillor Simons and his business partner Mr Arch. Near the spot where Mr Temple fell was the poignant sight of a dead dog, and there were bloodstains from hands and heads on the rocks all around. When the *Lord of the Isles* hoved into view from Inveraray, the remaining passengers were met by the shocking sight of bodies and bloodied men, women and children, some staggering drunkenly as they came to from the effects of the gases.

Most of the councillors had been overcome by the fumes, hats had been lost in the quarry and all were filthy. Two doctors – Wilson and Nelson – had been among the passengers who were overcome, but they now helped to take the dead and injured on board the steamer. Dr Campbell, the Inveraray doctor who had been on his rounds at Crarae, also went on board to help. Telegrams were handed in at Tighnabruaich and Rothesay to ask for two ambulance wagons to meet the boat and for funeral undertakers Messrs Wylie and Lochhead to arrange to take the bodies from Greenock to Glasgow.

The news, therefore, went ahead of the arrival of the *Lord of the Isles* and her sorry cargo. A huge crowd was waiting at Princes Pier and there was a struggle to get Bailie Young, Councillor J. H. Martin, Mr Harvey, and a reporter, Mr David Young, to the Greenock hospital. The story was in the evening papers before the survivors' train reached St Enoch's railway station and huge crowds met them when they reached Glasgow. The Rev. Mr Stewart, who was Matthew Waddell's minister, had been asked to break the news to Mrs Waddell and the family, but Bailie Campbell had already done so. Mr Waddell had also been a personal friend of Mr Steel, so both families experienced a double loss.

The focus of concern lay in the city, yet a number of people from Crarae had also been overcome by the fumes. It did not seem to occur to anyone to take them on board the steamer to be treated at Greenock Infirmary, but fortunately they recovered. A report that three shepherds up in the hills behind Crarae had also been affected by the blast was said by the *Oban Times* to be 'incorrect'.

This 'monster blast' was the last at the Crarae quarry; work was not resumed. On Tuesday, 28 September, Her Majesty's Inspector of Explosives, Colonel A. Ford, and Argyllshire's chief constable began an investigation into the disaster and a report was delivered to the Secretary of State for the Home Department the following year. The content of that report did not, of course, suggest that there were malevolent spirits within the boulders which crashed to the quarry floor that September weekend in 1886: there was a scientific reason for the deaths of seven people and the poisoning of so many more. But perhaps another explanation might have been given by the people of Kilneuair, who believed the boulders in the walls of their church – transported as they had been across the moors from Crarae – were haunted by souls unreleased from Purgatory.

The skills of modern archaeologists are now conspiring to prove that at least part of this curious tale of the Loch Fyne stones contains some truth. In the late 1950s, plans were drawn up to build a storage dam for the North of Scotland Hydro-Electric Board which was to raise the level of water in Loch Glashan in the upland basin behind Loch Gair by about 45 feet. However, while the engineers were working to find a firm foundation for this dam, the level of the loch was actually lowered by about 9 feet. This exposed a width of former beach and lacustrine silts out in the loch, and the engineers recognised that on what had been a small island in a previous age, there was the site of a crannog.

In 1960, as much of Mid Argyll waited for its first electricity supply, a team of archaeologists was called in under the direction of Mr and Mrs J. G. Scott, who were based at Glasgow University. The Scotts found sherds of medieval pottery in the silts, and evidence of a dugout canoe

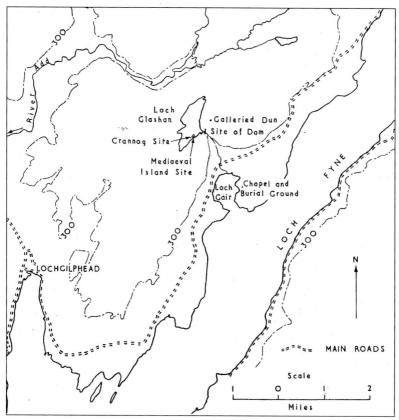

Glashan Loch was examined by archaeologists before the hydro
scheme proceeded. *Society of Antiquaries of Scotland.*

was discovered where a causeway had linked the island settlement to
the mainland. The archaeologists were working against the clock. This
island was soon to be submerged under about 30 feet of water for the
sake of progress, and, for three weeks in late July and early August 1961,
the Scotts brought in Horace Fairhurst, Gordon Petrie, Euan Mackie
and some university students to try to salvage as many artefacts and as
much knowledge of this medieval site as possible before it was drowned.
It was a wet three weeks and there were regrets that more could not be
done. But a paper written by Horace Fairhurst, MA PhD, and published
with the aid of a grant from the Carnegie Trust for the Universities of
Scotland, holds possible clues to the curious circumstances surrounding
Kilneuair and the stones of Loch Fyne.

What was discovered was remarkable. On the island – which had been about 150 feet long from north-north-east to south-south-west, and 50 feet across – overlooking the causeway, there was a terrace on which the experts found the outlines of five rectangular buildings and a pen-like enclosure. The buildings were from different periods and lying on the ground was an almost complete semicircular stone-cut archway which looked as if it might be from a chapel door. According to Horace Fairhurst, this archway could have given rise to a local tradition that the island had been the site of a monastery.

The problem was that there was no other evidence that monks had ever been established on or around Loch Glashan. A nearby galleried dun, some old field dykes and two ruinous dry-stone cottages were all that had ever been found in the immediate area, and the ruins of the chapel of St Bride to the north of Loch Gair gave no hint of any monastic activity in the neighbourhood. Yet here, lying within the entrance area of two medieval buildings were the remains of a stone-cut arch: a large and a small fragment which fitted together to form an almost complete semicircle of 3 feet 6 inches across – 'rebated as for a door and carved with remarkable precision from a rough block of schist', according to Horace Fairhurst. Near the arch lay a silver penny of the time of Edward II (1307–27). Also found on the site was a half groat from the reign of Robert II (1370–90). Some carefully trimmed and tooled corner stones matching the craftsmanship of the arch were found in the walls of the largest building on the terrace, and a slab which may have been an incomplete piece of sculpture, perhaps intended as a crucifixion scene, was built into the base of the wall. Cannibalisation of previous constructions for a subsequent generation of buildings has always taken place in Argyll, regardless of any venerable attribution.

The archaeologists were persuaded that the arch, the jamb stones and the sculpture had been made for a chapel – particularly so when they found that there was a very similar stone arch above the south door in the ruinous church of Kilmory in the Craignish peninsula, 11 miles to the north-west on the Mid Argyll seaward coast. The team was convinced that these extraneous stones were out of place in the fourteenth-century buildings on the Loch Glashan island, and Horace Fairhurst records in his paper that 'It has been suggested to us that the wrought stones can be linked with a tradition mentioned in the *New Statistical Account*, written in 1844. Speaking of Kilneuair church near the south-west end of Loch

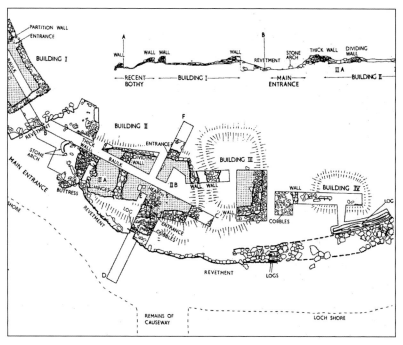

Excavation plan at Glashan Loch. *Society of Antiquaries of Scotland.*

Awe, the account of the Parish of Glassary states . . .' Here, Fairhurst
goes on to quote the passage about the stones dressed in Killevin and
passed from man to man across the 12 miles to Kilneuair. Dr Fairhurst
also quotes from a different source which gives another twist to the tradition. In *Origines Parochiales Scotiae* (1854) it says 'The church appears
to have stood originally at Killevin near Crarae on Lochfyne where a
burial ground still remains, and to have afterwards been removed to
Kilneuair on Loch Awe where there is still a ruined church.' A note in
the same edition adds, 'The church at Kilneuair is said to have been
built of stones quarried and dressed close to Killevin, a tradition which
seems to intimate the building of the one church from the materials
of the other.'

As Dr Fairhurst points out in his paper, 'As the crow flies, the distance
from Killevin near Crarae to Kilneuair is well under twelve miles, but
the nearest practical route for such a transfer of hewn stones would seem
to have been firstly along the coast to Loch Gair, and thence by a twelve
mile land route via Loch Glashan to the River Add, and so to Loch Awe.'

Scientist though he was, he was loath to dismiss the potentially 'improbable' tradition. The fact that there was no ready explanation for the presence of the wrought stones on the Glashan island and their presence on a logical route for stones to travel between Killevin and Kilneuair was an equation he could not totally condemn as flawed.

Any possible conclusive evidence was submerged in the weeks after the archaeological team left, and the surrounding countryside is now swamped by a sea of conifers planted by the Forestry Commission. It is, of course, possible that there had been plans in the late fourteenth or early fifteenth century for a church on the island which were abandoned after some stones were dressed by craftsmen – Fairhurst suggests masons at the Cistercian Abbey of Saddell in Kintyre might have been employed. This, Dr Fairhurst allowed in his paper, is not backed by any documentation. The curious carrying of the stones from Loch Fyne to Loch Awe, however, is a story heavily weighted by tradition and even given some credence by the Kirk.

But how did the Devil get into the story of the stones? Was it Auld Nick who scared the cross-legged braggadocio? Was it some force of evil which caused the Crarae quarry tragedy? On 7 February 1956, a lady who signed herself Mrs W. Ross wrote to the *Oban Times* about the Devil's handprint on the door jamb at Kilneuair. She had been at a lecture about the church and when the famous claw marks were mentioned, a

Stone arch, perhaps destined for Kilneuair Church, found at Glashan Loch. *Society of Antiquaries of Scotland.*

Kilneuair's eighteenth-century oratory, *c.* 1880. © *Royal Commission on the Ancient and Historical Monuments of Scotland.*

voice behind her said, 'I am the devil who made the mark.' This may have sent a lesser woman scurrying from the lecture hall with the same haste that the tailor left Kilneuair church; Mrs Ross, however, was made of sterner stuff. She stayed to chat with the 'devil' over tea and scones at the end of the lecture and learned that when this gentleman, whose name was Gregor McGregor, was a young lad, masons had been asked to look at the ruins and if possible to find the stone with the Devil's fingerprints. Mr McGregor told Mrs Ross that no such stone could be found, 'but the masons were quite willing to produce one'. All hands were measured and the journeyman with the biggest was chosen to make the mark. Mr McGregor was that journeyman. He died in Lochgilphead in 1952 at the age of ninety-two, placing the handprint prank in the early 1870s.

Kilneuair is now a pretty ruin. The Crarae quarry which killed seven people and a dog a decade or so after Gregor McGregor was drawing his fingernails down a newly screed door jamb was closed on 20 December 1890 and is today the dramatic backdrop to a cafe which serves tourists who arrive by road rather than by steamer. Are these 21st-century visitors

curious about the quarry? Does the singular medieval arch in the wall of
the Hydro Electric plant a few miles along the road from Crarae, with its
explanatory plaque about the archaeological find at Loch Glashan, stir
their interest? Despite advances in geology and archaeology, the secrets
of the stones of Loch Fyneside remain as tantalisingly curious as ever.

2

THE LAIRD, HIS LADY AND THE
LEAD MINES

In Celtic times there was an almost spiritual connection with the land, and from it grew the concept of the land being in the guardianship of those who worked it, rather than being the property of a landowner. The medieval Scottish kings granted charters to the most powerful clan chiefs which gave them dominion over sometimes immense tracts of land; but the people who lived within their boundaries owed their loyalty to the clan chief more because of blood ties than because he was their landlord. There were, of course, demands made of the crofters and fishermen: 'fencible men' – those who were fit and able to fight – were obliged to follow the standard of their chief when called to do so, and to furnish the chief's household with barley, oats, cheese and other produce. On the other hand, the laird kept a roof over his crofters' heads. The system held its benefits for both.

This feudal order – which was, of course, abused by some and made exemplary by others – lasted until the end of the British Civil Wars of the seventeenth century. In some cases, it could be said to have gone on long beyond the Union of the Parliaments in 1707, but the devastating effects of the previous century's civil wars meant that many 'heritors' – those who, like the earls of Argyll and their cadet families around the county, had inherited the land through the family line – were all but wiped out financially. And those who had not been ruined by the British Civil Wars managed to do the job themselves by investing hugely in the ill-fated Darien Scheme, which was promoted as a new Scottish colony with huge potential for returns on investment. Instead, it turned out to be Scotland's answer to England's South Sea Bubble, and it saw the country's hopes of regaining fortunes evaporate like the morning mist steaming off the tropical forests on the isthmus of Panama.

As the eighteenth century progressed, more and more heritors found that the only answer to their financial problems was to sell off great tracts of their land. The gifts of medieval kings were put up for auction or placed in questionable trusts. And so it was that parcels of Scotland were sold off to Lowlanders and to Englishmen, who wanted returns for their investments. Few felt responsible for the families living on their newly acquired properties, viewing them only as rent-paying tenants who must create a profit or face eviction. As with the traditional heritors before them, there were good and bad in the mix, but the situation led to some very curious landlords – and very curious developments in unlikely corners of Argyll.

Sir David Murray of Stanhope bought into Argyll early in this 'modern' era of the county's history. A 2nd baronet, he had been the MP for Peeblesshire from 1681 to 1682 and again in 1689. He was a wealthy man, owning much property in the Borders, including the baronies of Broughton and Stobo and other lands in the parishes of Drumelzier and Tweedsmuir. Around 1723 – the family history dates and the *Statistical Account* records do not tally – he bought the lands of Ardnamurchan. Although he was a Lowlander, he was also a Jacobite and had actively supported the cause in the 1715 Uprising. His neighbours in the Borders were Covenanters through and through but his allegiance to the Jacobite cause would have won approval on his new estate in Argyll. There, the local people still hankered after a throne occupied by a descendant of James VII and II, who had been pushed into abdicating in 1688, rather than the Hanoverian offspring of the line of James VI and I's daughter Elizabeth, who had married the King of Bavaria and was known as the 'Winter Queen'. Even though Sir David would not consent to conspire to cause rebellion against the government after the 1715 Uprising, this was a man whose heart openly lay with the princes over the water and he promised to draw his sword on their behalf if the chance arose again.

Not so his son Alexander, the third of Sir David's thirteen children and the oldest male to survive, who succeeded to the title when Sir David died at his lodging in the Canongate parish of Edinburgh in 1729. Sir David Murray was a product of the seventeenth century, but his son Alexander was a man of his own time. He was born in 1687, the year before the Catholic James VII and II had been put off the throne in favour of the Protestant William and Mary, and by the time the Hanoverian George came to reign over these islands in 1714, Alexander had learned to blow with whatever wind was favourable to his own self interest, rather than to play politics. Perhaps having been born into a new era convinced young Alexander to support the Hanoverian incumbents who succeeded in 1714, but his support may have been cemented when he met a young Borders lady named Grisell Baillie, whom he courted earnestly but perhaps, as we shall see, unwisely. She was the daughter of George Baillie of Jerviswood and Lady Grizel Hume, the daughter of the Covenanting Earl of Marchmont and a poet and ballad writer renowned in her native Peeblesshire. Young Grisell had aspirations to be more than a wife and mother herself, and she took up her pen to write a memoir of her mother.

Despite Alexander's family status and his role as MP for Peeblesshire, George Baillie was not pleased with the proposed marriage and it took much persuasion by 'Grissie' to achieve a reluctant consent. When the couple did eventually marry, in 1710, Sir David Murray gave his son the baronies of Stanhope and Broughton.

In 1720 Sir Alexander was given custody of the Ardnamurchan and Sunart properties. From a modern perspective, this might seem remark-able; however, according to the *Statistical Account* of 1845, Alexander was an 'extraordinary man, whose sagacity readily discovered the chief

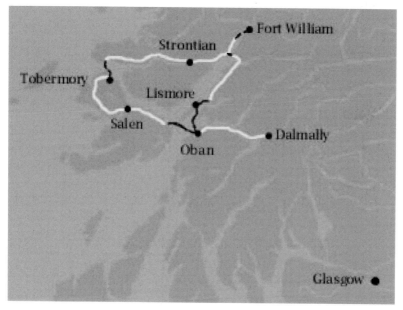

The Ardnamurchan area was sold to the Murrays of Stanhope, a Border family, at the start of the eighteenth century (white shows land routes and black, sea routes).

points of civil and industrial improvement of which these lands were perceptible'. In other words, he spotted the potential of the land and minerals in the area and set about exploiting it.

He began well, using the soundest market and social research techniques to help him plan his new business venture. He took a detailed census of the population and the stock and had surveys done of all resources, above and below ground. The estates were scientifically mapped out; Loch Sunart was charted by a Lieutenant Bruce, with notes and plans added by Alexander Murray himself, which included the building of harbours and the draining and irrigation of the land.

This was a time when lairds around Scotland were looking south and seeing the improvements which modern methods of drainage, irrigation and the enclosure of land could bring. They began to consolidate townships, giving to one tenant land that had been worked by four or five families. Alexander began draining and irrigating the difficult Ardnamurchan territory on 'an immense scale'. He also leased land at Strontian that contained lead deposits to the York Building Company, which had as its senior partner Edward Duke of Norfolk, with shares held by Alexander Murray himself, Sir Alexander Grant of Monymusk and General George Wade. Alexander claimed, or certainly is today acknowledged by the Strontian Mining Company, to have discovered the mineral wealth himself in 1722 when a substantial deposit of lead ore was identified at what is today known as the Strontian Mines. Local wisdom gave them a much longer history and the local people saw the mines as their own. However, Alexander Murray's takeover and the development of the mines by the York Building Company meant that they were worked on a commercial basis – something which the earls of Argyll had rarely had the finances to do, and perhaps seldom the time or inclination.

The natives of Ardnamurchan soon became aware that Murray did not have their welfare in mind. While the mines brought huge employment to the area, there was no access to prosperity for the local people. Instead, some 500 skilled workers were drafted in from England and a village named New York was built to house them, made from timber frames constructed in London.

Curiously enough, while the stereotypical mine worker is rough, ready and rowdy, the minister reported in the *Statistical Account* that it was the settlers who introduced hitherto unknown 'arts of peace' to the 'warlike Highlanders'. These 'arts of peace', however, were not taken

Mingary Castle, where Sir Alexander Murray took up residence.

on board in their entirety by the people of Ardnamurchan. Alexander's presence was not liked: there was resentment that so many workers had been imported from England. Furthermore, Alexander's presence in Ardnamurchan replaced one Covenanter – the Earl of Argyll, who had sold the land to the Murrays – with another – this one a Lowlander – in an area which would in the next quarter of the century show its loyalties to the Stuarts in no uncertain terms, and as Alexander's overt support of the Hanoverians became clear to the mainly Jacobite supporters, their dislike was confirmed.

People were not slow to make a statement about their Lawlan' landlord and soon he was to hear that his new tenants were stealing cattle, throwing sheep over precipices and setting fire to buildings to such an extent that General Wade was asked to send in a sergeant and twenty men with a warrant allowing them to use firearms if necessary – all in an effort to protect the property. This was not Highland hospitality: it was sabotage.

With many resources being channelled towards the welfare of the expert imported workforce at the mines, and open hostility to Alexander's ideas of farm enclosure, things did not progress smoothly. In his 'Second Report to the Commissioners and Trustees for Improving Fisheries and Manufactures in Scotland', Richard Neilson described a journey through

Ardnamurchan made in the 1750s, a few short years after Sir Alexander Murray's death. The road was bad and the terrain was rough and mountainous but the 'grassings' – the pasture available to cattle on what was by then 'part of the Sequestrated Estate of Sir Charles Murray of Stanhope' (Alexander's heir) – was 'esteemed among the best' in the Highlands. Yet Neilson said that the mutton which was available in the area was very bad because the fresh meat was sold to the mines at Strontian and to ships which called in on their way through the Sound of Mull. This must have been the case from the outset of the development of the mine.

Despite the unrest, and despite his penchant for gambling – or what the *Statistical Account* called his 'over-speculative and sanguine temperament' – Alexander could probably have kept things on an even keel if he had not come to his new estate with the burden of financial responsibilities elsewhere weighing heavily on his shoulders. The previous landlord, the Duke of Argyll, had been forced to sell up because a war, a revolution and a couple of executions had exhausted the family coffers; Alexander Murray came to Ardnamurchan under a very curious, but no less financially draining, set of circumstances, particularly in view of the Catholic morals of his new tenants. Simply put, his marriage to Grisell had not simply been a failure, it had actually ended in divorce. For his tenants, losing one's head for a cause was acceptable, but losing one's wife in a law court was not. For Alexander himself, the burden of the divorce settlement was taxing.

Alexander claimed, possibly with justification, that Grisell was unfaithful. Was the ballad which Grisell's friend Lady Mary Worley Montagu wrote about an adventure Grisell was said to have shared with her footman Arthur Grey simply romantic nonsense, or grounds for the divorce? Whatever the truth, the couple's marriage ended in an acrimonious legal wrangle, with Grisell counterclaiming that Sir Alexander 'under a pleasing exterior possessed a dark, moody, and ferocious temper amounting almost to insanity, which made him the helpless victim of the most groundless suspicions'.

Grisell obtained a decree of separation and aliment against him on 15 March 1714, and she went back to live at her father's house, where no doubt the phrase 'I told you so' was hanging heavily in the air. These were the days of marriage settlements, particularly among the wealthy and the titled, and just like any modern divorce, agreement had to be reached on who would take what from the marriage.

Grisell, Lady Murray, daughter of a Covenanting family in the Borders. Her marriage to Sir Alexander Murray of Stanhope ended in the divorce court. *Mellerstain Collection. Photographed by John Haddington.*

The wrangling over the settlement rumbled on well into the years of Alexander's proprietorship in Ardnamurchan. Grisell had brought a 'tocher' or dowry of 20,000 merks to the marriage and Alexander settled on her by deed on 22 September 1720 an aliment of £150, payable from the lands and barony of Stobo. Despite the discovery and extraction of the minerals in Ardnamurchan, this aliment was not paid and Grisell raised an action to claim the Stobo property from her former husband in 1727; she was given a Crown charter of adjudication on 12 February 1729 which enabled her to sign over her rights and claims to her father, who carried on the fight. Two years later, Sir Alexander had to hand over to Baillie his lands and barony of Stobo, as well as those of Stanhope

Murray, Over and Nether Menzion, Glenrath and others. Had he not already sold the lands and barony of Broughton to John Douglas, brother of William, Earl of March, in 1719, he would no doubt have lost those to his former father-in-law as well. Perhaps she did not quite take him for every penny he had, but Grisell certainly did not help his financial situation, and although the mines at Strontian were worked from 1724 to 1740, when Alexander died on 18 May 1743 he was, according to Keith W. Murray in his book *Murray Pedigrees,* in financial ruin. He left little more than a title to the nephew who succeeded him. His heir, Sir David Murray, was the son of his brother David, a wine merchant in Leith.

Grisell Baillie Murray died on 6 June 1759, perhaps in some material comfort, leaving behind her enough tittle-tattle to further besmirch her former husband's memory. She raised the question of his sanity by repeating stories her friends and allies had told her to fuel her evidence in the divorce courts. According to the *Household Book of Lady Grisell Baillie*, Alexander Murray of Stanhope lurked around the studio where, some time after the divorce, she was having her portrait painted, standing for 'an hour with his arms folded gazing at her likeness'. Some women would have been touched and perhaps regretful that their cast-off husband would want to look at their portrait; Grisell used it as evidence of Alexander's obsessiveness and jealousy.

3

MINISTERS

Some of the most momentous events in history have been sparked by the smallest of actions, taken by the most obscure of people, in the most insignificant of places. The Judas kiss, the assassination of the Archduke in Sarajevo, the message delivered to Mingary Castle: each led to unthinkable consequences. While the first two instances are instantly recognisable as respectively the delivery of Christ into the hands of the authorities who would crucify Him and the catalyst for the commencement of the First World War, the significance of the third action curiously remains almost as obscure as it seemed on the August night in 1745* when it was executed. Yet this action had repercussions which some would argue continue to affect a nation and its people to this day. It was an action which led to slaughter on the battlefield, butchery of civilians and the proscription of a culture. It changed the politics of Britain. It created myth and romantic legend. It multiplied the Scottish diaspora a thousandfold. And it was carried out by a man of the cloth whose parishioners could not conceal the fire kindled in them by the near presence of a foreigner dressed as a scruffy seminarian.

Lachlan Campbell arrived on the Ardnamurchan peninsula in 1737, openly loyal to the 'Protestant Succession' manipulated in 1688 by, among others, the then Earl of Argyll. Although the earl's successor had sold off parts of the Ardnamurchan lands, he was still Campbell's ultimate employer – as he was of many of Lachlan's parishioners. The minister and his parishioners did not see eye to eye in a political sense – but then, Ardnamurchan had not had much luck with its ministers for more than a century prior to Lachlan's arrival. It is a curious fact that for more than a century after the first recorded account of a minister in the area, the word 'controversy' could be said to have aptly applied to almost all of Ardnamurchan's men of the cloth.

*All dates in this chapter are according to the Old Calendar, which was altered in the mid eighteenth century.

Comgan came from Ireland at the end of the seventh century, and
traces of Cill Comhghan (Comgan's Cell) can be seen beneath the
near wall in this image of the medieval chapel of Kilchoan.

Of course, although Ardnamurchan's Kirk records do not begin until 1624, this most westerly point of the British Isles was no stranger
to religion before that. Perhaps it had been even better suited to the
Celtic Christianity which St Columba brought when he was travelling
east to spread the Word, at a time when the kingdom of Dalriada was
a powerful entity, well established from modern-day Kintyre to Appin.
Beyond, taking in the Ardnamurchan peninsula, was land ruled by the
Northern Picts. There were battles over the no-man's-land in between
the two territories in the decade or so after Columba arrived at Iona,
but he seemed to pass safely through Ardnamurchan on his missionary
journey east from that island into mainland Scotland. Columba and his
companions stopped at Ardslignish, a point on the Ardnamurchan coast
west of what would become Kilchoan, and the well there was named
after him. A farm above Camus-nan-Geall, a little bay near Ardslignish,
is called 'heavenly' (Muirbulg of neamh) in Adomnan's *Life of Columba*,
but 'rough and rocky' are the two adjectives which seem to have sprung
most readily to the saint's lips to describe the rest of the peninsula. Some

of the local people were converted by Columba, and their faith may have been nurtured a century or so later in the late 600s or early 700s when still more Irish missionaries arrived and Comhghan, or Comgan, stayed on in Ardnamurchan and built a place of worship there. Kilchoan is a corruption of the Gaelic Cill Comhghan and there are traces in the grounds of the old parish church of that early holy place.

There is not much evidence of the priestly personalities who shared their lives with the people of Aird-nam-moo-chuan (promontory of the great or of the narrow seas, depending which translation is chosen) in the five centuries during which the Norsemen held sway. Tyrants such as Muchdragon MacRi Lochlunn, who continued to rule Ardnamurchan even after the Battle of Largs in 1263 saw power return to the Scots, were in legend at least known for libertine rather than pious behaviour. And although the influence of the saintly Queen Margaret stretched as far as Ardnamurchan, there was little peace there in which to enjoy religion. The Lord of the Isles, the all-powerful John of Islay, who ruled all these western territories as if he were a king, was an aggressive overlord, and although his lands were eventually taken from him, the clans native to Ardnamurchan – the MacIans, MacLeans and MacDonalds – then squabbled within the peninsula for centuries, with the Campbells inevitably entering the fray in a major way in the early 1600s. This Campbell influence meant that the people of Sunart and Ardnamurchan became at least nominally Protestant, while those living to the north under Clanranald remained Catholic.

The MacIans seem to have finally lost their lands to the Campbells because of the actions of a woman who resigned her rights as a MacIan heiress in favour of one of the earls of Argyll. In 1612, Archibald, 4th Earl of Argyll, sent Donald Campbell of Barbreck to Ardnamurchan to take up these rights and engender income through rents. This emissary was as tyrannical as any Norseman of the previous millennium and John Clanranald from neighbouring Moidart came south to help the people throw Donald Campbell out of the area in 1618. Sadly, he was soon back with government approval – the earl had great influence at this time – and again he bled the people dry. In 1624 the people revolted against Campbell and more than a hundred of the MacIans took to the high seas as pirates, wreaking revenge on the Campbell lands the length of the west coast – not to mention indulging in a little indiscriminate plundering.

It was in that same year, while the MacIans were busy terrorising the west coast in a last attempt to get their lands back from the Campbells, and the Campbells were putting any remaining MacIans in Ardnamurchan to the sword, that the first record of a minister in Ardnamurchan was made. Donald Omey's ministry centred upon the little medieval chapel of St Comgan at Kilchoan, but his parish was dauntingly widespread. Curiously, despite the Protestant influence of the Campbells, Omey was a Celtic Catholic. He had been sent there by Andrew Boyd, Bishop of Argyll, not only to save souls but to quell the fighting between the Campbells, MacIans and Clanranalds. Resentful of the ploy, the Chief of Clanranald sent a letter to Fr Omey, which was delivered to him in the pulpit by a messenger dressed more for a skirmish on the battlefield than a Sabbath service. The sword, targe and musket made it clear to Omey that Clanranald's threat on his life if he did not leave Ardnamurchan immediately was more than picturesque speech.

When Omey left, Sir Donald Campbell put in his own man, Duncan McCalman, a Protestant. Mr McCalman, according to Father Charles MacDonald, the parish priest in Moidart in the second half of the nineteenth century, 'had to preach to empty benches'. In his book *Moidart: or Among the Clanranalds*, he says that that the 'Maclachlans and Hendersons remained outside the church amusing themselves by *putting* the stone. But the minister was equal to the occasion. He could *put* the stone too, and to some effect, for he *put* it farther than any of them.' With the fine irony of a man who knew the difficulties of maintaining a parish, Fr Macdonald concluded, 'A pastor who could do this was clearly deserving of a congregation', and after that initial battle of wills, Mr McCalman kept his congregation for many years.

The old adage that one should never mix politics and religion never seemed to be applied in Ardnamurchan, and trouble came Mr McCalman's way during the British Civil Wars. In 1644 Alastair MacDonald, son of the infamous Coll Ciotach, took three Covenanting ministers hostage. When MacDonald brought his hostages – Mr and Mrs Weir, Mr Hamilton and Mr Watson – to the peninsula on his way from Ireland with 1,500 men to join the Duke of Montrose, Mr McCalman seems to have been less than censorious. The ministers were held in Mingary Castle and used by MacDonald as pawns to bargain for the release of prisoners from his side. Mrs Weir was released on 3 September, but the ministers were kept in the castle on rations of barley-meal and muddy rainwater. Mr Weir died at the start of the winter and Mr Watson in the March of 1645. Only after interventions by the General Assembly of the Church of Scotland and the Scottish Parliament was Mr Hamilton released on 2 May 1645 in exchange for prisoners.

It is hard to judge a man's actions out of his time. Suffice to say that Mr McCalman's apparent complicity in the keeping of the hostages was seen by his Church in 1650 as worthy of excommunication. He was re-instated by the Presbytery in 1672, but he died soon after. His death did not, however, break the run of bad luck experienced by the peninsula's parishioners: his replacement continued the curious run of controversial Ardnamurchan ministers. Martin McIlvra had been excommunicated two years before he took over from McCalman because he had sided with the rebels, but this seems to have been overlooked in 1650. A Gaelic speaker, he translated the Book of Nehemiah into his congregation's native tongue, but in 1658 he went absent without leave for ten weeks and landed in trouble again. He was also rebuked for 'gross unchristian claims', a charge which seems to have been the straw which snapped the church authorities' clemency. Mr McIlvra was turned out from the Ardnamurchan church without a penny. The £100 compensation he was later awarded did little to remedy his downfall and he died a poor man in 1687.

As the bloody century of civil war came to an end and society began to change, it might be imagined that the parishioners of Ardnamurchan would experience some well-deserved peace. Not so. They became very fond of Alexander MacDonald, the next minister at Kilchoan, but he was an Episcopalian who refused to become a Presbyterian after the Act of Settlement. From 1697 he was not allowed to preach at Kilchoan and instead looked after his flock from Eilean Finain until his death in 1724. Meanwhile, in 1700 there was an attempt to introduce a minister by the name of John McCalman – unrelated to the previous McCalman incumbent – and the saga of unsuitability, rejection and farce continued. This Mr McCalman was barred from the Kilchoan church by the congregation, even when he turned up in full Highland dress in an attempt to mollify a people whose lands, language, culture and heritage had been trampled underfoot during the seventeenth century.

James Stevenson was the minister during the 1715 Uprising, and after he left, in February 1732, yet another disaster was waiting in the wings in the form of one Daniel MacLauchlan. In 1733, Mr MacLauchlan had been charged with intemperance, profanity and singing indecent songs

– not the ideal activities for a minster. The charges were, however, found not proven in August 1733 and the following month he was ordained at Kilchoan. In the November he left, to re-emerge some nine months later in King's Bench Prison in London, where he was held on suspicion of having written an obscene pamphlet – an essay entitled 'Improving and Adding to the Strength of Great Britain and Ireland by Fornication'.

This run of inappropriate incumbents was by no means at an end. The people of Ardnamurchan could have been forgiven had they turned their backs altogether on an institution which had offered anything but shepherds to care for their pastoral needs. The blame, of course, could not be laid solely at the door of the Kirk. These were still troubled times and the people who held secular power also wielded power within religious spheres. It is useful to remember that in the years after King William of Orange and his wife Mary were imported from Holland as an alternative to James VII and II of England, the Earl of Breadalbane received £20,000 from the government – not such an enormous sum given the complete devastation of the landscape and of clan economies – to sweeten the clan chiefs in favour of William and help them forget the Stuarts. Peerages or lump sums were on offer in return for allegiance oaths, but perhaps more persuasive were Sir John Dalrymple's death threats to those who seemed unlikely to come on board. After the 1715 Uprising, sweeteners were no longer an option and English troops were garrisoned in areas where Stuart support was strongest. Resentment brewed.

It is not surprising then that when Charles Edward Stuart decided in 1745 to make a bid for the throne he believed was rightfully his, he chose to seek support in areas such as Ardnamurchan and Moidart.

Many experts have pontificated on the inevitable failure of the 1745 rising. They have accused Charles Edward Stuart of delivering thousands into the barbarous hands of the Duke of Cumberland, not to mention failing to forsee the banning of the plaid, the abolition of the heritable jurisdictions of the clan chiefs and the social breakdown of the clan system. Hindsight is, however, a great gift. The Stuart prince in fact had good reason for believing he could succeed, and the aftermath of the 1715 Uprising had not been overly severe. In his biography of Charles Edward Stuart, Frank McLynn suggests that it was a rational assumption that rebellion in Scotland in 1745 would be an incentive to the French to finish off the weak Hanoverian monarchy in London. There is also no doubt that, for a whole range of reasons, many Scots were agin the English, even if they were not for the prince over the water. The 1707 Act of Union was still unpopular. There were demonstrations in Glasgow and Edinburgh against harsh taxes. In the north-east, Catholics and Episcopalians supported the Stuarts and there was strong Jacobite feeling still in the Highlands where clan chiefs held no truck with the government's interference in land-holding traditions. As we have seen, in Ardnamurchan the people had been given no motivation to support the Hanoverians: had they not just experienced two decades of watching a man enclosing their crofts and bringing in outsiders to work his mines? Sir Alexander Murray's actions, which forced many to migrate to the cities or across the Atlantic, were already being replicated by landlords throughout the Highlands and Islands.

There were concrete factors which boded well for an uprising, too. Troops which had been garrisoned in Scotland since 1715 were now fighting in Continental Europe. In Argyll, the Hanoverian Campbells were unable to muster the large numbers of fencible men which had

Prince Charles Edward Stuart had the support of the people of Ardnamurchan.

previously been at their beck and call because the 2nd Duke had made his own revolutionary leap from feudalism to capitalism. His brother had since inherited the title and begun to reverse these modern moves, but the Jacobite prince's intelligence sources must have reported in 1744 that this reversal was not far enough advanced to pose much of a threat to the proposed uprising. Thus it was that the *Elisabeth* and the *Du Teillay* sailed on a prayer and a fair wind for Scotland in July1745.

It was not plain sailing. The English were aware of the plot and Captain Brett on HMS *Lion* caught up with the two ships 100 miles west of the Cornish Lizard. The *Elisabeth* was a premier-class warship and did plenty of damage to the *Lion*, but she was unable to continue her voyage as the enemy ship headed back to Plymouth. It was too risky to transfer the 1,500 muskets and 1,800 broadswords, and the Jacobite men from the *Elisabeth* to the *Du Teillay*, and at 11 o'clock at night on 20 July, the *Du Teillay* had to make a solitary and ill-equipped journey towards Scotland. Enemy ships, high seas and low morale made this a long and unhappy voyage. The ship eventually reached the island of Barra, and, with the help of a boatman taking his cattle between the islands, she was piloted to Eriskay on 23 July. The prince's ally on Mull, Sir Hector Maclean, was now in custody, so the onward destination was changed to Moidart – an area which was remote and difficult for government troops but easily negotiated by the Catholic, pro-Jacobite Clanranald men. Unfortunately, while the prince rested on Eriskay in the guise of a seminarian from the Scots college in Rome, news came from South Uist that two Skye chiefs were unwilling to join the rebellion because of the lack of promised French troops. He was advised to go home. The prince told Boisdale, 'I am come home', and he headed for Moidart nonetheless. On 25 July, the Pretender entered Loch-nam-Uamh and with the *Du Teillay* anchored at Lochailort in Arisaig, he found lodgings with a MacDonald in a Borrodale farmhouse.

His reception from local leaders was not entirely warm. The son of the Chief of the Clanranald MacDonalds suggested he go back to Rome. The Skye chiefs, MacLeod and Sir Alexander MacDonald, again refused to do anything without the promised 7,000 French troops. Word came in the following days from other supposedly supportive clan chiefs around Scotland, responding negatively to the call to arms. Charles Edward then played to the gallery. He ordered arms and ammunition to be offloaded from the *Du Teillay* before appealing directly to young Ranald

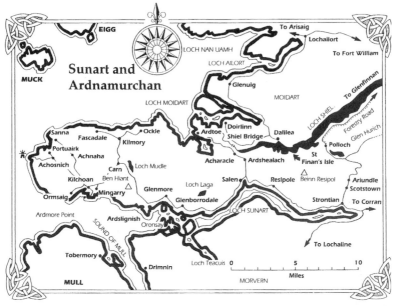

This map shows the arduous journey the minister had to make to
the church in the north of the peninsula and the closeness of the
bay where the prince's boat was anchored.

MacDonald. The gamble on charisma worked and Ranald declared
– admittedly after much much soul-searching in another room of the
Borrodale farmhouse – that he would follow his 'rightful prince'. This
set the ball rolling and other chiefs pledged to form an army.

While the top-level negotiations continued, at grassroots level the
support for the prince was swelling. The people, who lived in hovels
and survived on fish, oatmeal, barley and whey, were convinced that a
rebellion was for the best. The word that the unshaven student cleric
receiving secret visits from the high and mighty was in fact the Jacobite
prince did not have to spread far south-west from Loch-nam-Uamh to
reach Ardnamurchan. The rumour spread by those on board the French
ship that she was smuggling brandy and could not find a buyer for the
expensive cargo was soon seen by the locals for the ruse it was. The tension was palpable. By the time people met in the churches at Kilmory
and Kilchoan they were on fire with the spirit of revolution.

Enter Lachlan Campbell, the minister of Ardnamurchan and Eilean
Finain in 1745. The parish at that time went beyond the peninsula and

into Arisaig. Every second Sunday, Mr Campbell had to make his way
from Kilchoan in the south-west corner of Ardnamurchan across 5 miles
of what St Columba had described as 'rough and rocky' terrain to the
church at Kilmory on the northern coast of the peninsula. Today a sin-
gle-track road and the combustion engine offer a degree of comfort to
the traveller; in 1745, the perilous path between boulder and bog must
have made these alternate Sabbath journeys arduous for the minister.
On 28 July he preached at Kilchoan and was aware that the Jacobites in
the congregation were edgy. On 4 August he set off for Kilmory, having prepared a sermon taken from St Paul's first epistle to Timothy. In
Chapter 2 of the King James version of the Bible, we hear St Paul exhort
'supplications, prayers, intercessions, and giving of thanks' for all men.
In Verse 2, he adds, 'For kings, and for all that are in authority; that we
may lead a quiet and peaceable life in all godliness and honesty.' A
modern translation cannot change the thrust of it. The Jerusalem Bible
of the late twentieth century says, 'My advice is that, first of all, there
should be prayers offered for everyone – petitions, intercessions and
thanksgiving – and especially for kings and others in authority, so that
we may be able to live religious and reverent lives in peace and quiet.' In
whatever way Mr Campbell developed this text, it could only be heard
as meaning one thing: pray for King George and his government and
don't even think of raising a squeak in favour of any alternative. The
minister was, after all, a Campbell, a Protestant, and he was openly loyal
to George II.

He had not set out to fan the flames. If the edginess he had witnessed
in Kilchoan the week before had given him pause for thought as he
penned his sermon, he did not at first suspect that the Pretender was no
more than 20 miles distant as the crow flies. The 3rd Duke of Argyll,
however, was not just Mr Campbell's clan chieftain, patron and indirect
landlord: he was also one of the governing giants in Scotland, responsible for policy and, as such, one of those who were 'in authority'. Lachlan
Campbell owed him the same loyalty as he owed King George and he no
doubt believed that this was as appropriate a time as any to remind the
people of Ardnamurchan, through the words of St Paul, that they also
should show some loyalty. When he reached Kilmory Church, however,
he again felt agitation in the air.

The little church – now rebuilt as a dwelling house – sat above sea level
with a fine panorama on view from its door, stretching from the islands

From the chapel at Kilmory, where the Rev. Lachlan Campbell preached every second Sunday, all eyes turned towards the place where Charles Edward's ship lay at anchor.

of Muck and Eigg in the north-west to Loch-nam-Uamh in the north-east. According to the Rev. Archibald Clark in the 1845 *New Statistical Account*, 'the church of Kilmorie was anciently of considerable extent; its foundations only can now be traced'. It was, he added, 'subjected to the fullest measure of the vengeance which rivalled the savage cruelty of the most barbarous age' – a vengeance which was set in motion by the Rev. Lachlan Campbell. He may have known that his parishioners in Kilmory were not in favour of King George, but until he felt the electricity among them and was told by one of them to beware of the consequences if he ever preached such a sermon again, he had no clue what was afoot on his doorstep. Now he made his way back to Kilchoan and met a parishioner whom he knew was not a Jacobite. According to the Annals of the Parish, the minister told Anna Cameron, 'I preached a sermon in Kilmory today and the people were like to go mad. I can take my oath upon it that the Pretender is in my parish.' Anna had been under oath to the prince's supporters to tell nothing 'until one could swear that he knew the Pretender was in Kinlochmoydart'. The minister's conviction caused her to let the cat out of the bag. She was able to tell Mr Campbell that the prince had six supporters with him and that word had been sent 'to all the chiefs about'.

Ifs and buts are words of no value, but if Lachlan Campbell had not preached his pro-Hanoverian sermon, if Anna Cameron had not confirmed his suspicions, and if Campbell had not sought out the Duke of Argyll's factor, Donald Campbell of Auchindoun, who was that Sunday night at Mingary Castle, and asked him to send a message to Inveraray, what might have become of the 1745 Uprising? As it was, Auchindoun dispatched a messenger from Mingary across Loch Sunart late that Sunday night as the last light was going down over the sea to the west. The word was passed to Donald Campbell of Airds, who sent urgently to the Sheriff-Depute of Argyll in Inveraray. The message, containing a greatly exaggerated report of the strength of Charles Edward's support, was received at 6 o'clock in the evening on Tuesday, 6 August. The Sheriff-Depute informed the Lord Justice Clerk and pre-emptive strikes against the Uprising were initiated almost before the clan chiefs had pledged their reluctant allegiance, and certainly long before London had woken up to the need to combat insurrection.

The history of the uprising and its aftermath is more than well documented, but the role of the Ardnamurchan minister in raising the alarm among the Scottish Hanoverians is curiously overlooked. The role of the

View south from Kilchoan church, where Lachlan Campbell first felt the tension in his parishioners; it was in this direction that his subsequent message was taken – to Inveraray and the Hanoverian authorities.

A faceless minister curiously changed the course of history with his sermon from the pulpit in Kichoan church.

parishioners in supporting Charles Edward was, however, not ignored after Culloden. The attention of the authorities must have seemed most unfair after so many centuries of neglect. In Volume 3 of the *Royal Commission on the Ancient and Historical Monuments of Scotland* we learn that a persistent shortage of clergy meant that the reformed church was less effective in Ardnamurchan than elsewhere in Argyll. Furthermore, 'adherence by several ministers in the 1640s and 1690s to the Royalist and Jacobite parties' obviously left its mark, as did the ministrations of Irish-Franciscan missionaries who travelled the western fringes of Scotland from the 1620s and claimed many converts.

The church at Kilmory is gone; only the view across to Loch-nam-Uamh remains unchanged. In Kilchoan, the church where Lachlan Campbell first felt the puzzlingly charged atmosphere is a picturesque roofless shell from which the Sound of Mull is viewed through windows framed by wild gooseberries and dog roses. Within the ruins there is evidence of a twelfth- or thirteenth-century church. The west gable wall incorporates a lot of medieval masonry, but the south wall was entirely reconstructed in the eighteenth century – probably when Kenneth MacCauley was transferred from the Isle of Harris to Kilchoan in 1761, five years after the death of Lachlan Campbell. The masonry is of random rubble with dressings of greenish-grey sandstone, which the Royal Commission suggests came from Lochaline. There is evidence that there were galleries in the church reached by internal timber staircases at the north-west and north-east corners. The pulpit from which Lachlan Campbell first felt the frisson of revolution was placed centrally on the north wall. In the churchyard where parishioners of a previous century had defined rebellion as *putting* the stone while the minister preached, there are medieval grave slabs – one depicting a cross and a birlinn, the other a birlinn in full sail, a stag, hounds and a huntsman with a long tassel on his hood – carved in the fourteenth to fifteenth century by craftsmen of the Iona School. The 'new' church, built in 1831 to a design by the fashionable architect William Burn, is at sufficient distance from the old to be free from the spirits of the past.

Bloodshed and misery are no strangers to Argyll, and one of its most remote parts has received more than its fair share. Ardnamurchan today can present itself as a peaceful haven or a challenging wilderness. The characters who have played on its stage throughout the centuries have ranged from the saintly to the tyrannical. The man who arguably caused the most negative impact on Ardnamurchan – and who changed the course of Scotland's history – was, however, curiously nondescript. A black-clad, faceless man whose gift was to read a mood and whose privilege it was to have the ear of his more important clansmen.

4

TRAMS, TUNNELS AND TRAINS

Argyll – for some, Tir nan Og, for others, the busy hub of local government, for others still, an area not quite meriting the investment of a ferry crossing to Ireland nor even the repair of a main trunk road. Today, 'remote' and 'isolated' are two of the words commonly used in conjunction with the long and straggling county, with its twenty-six inhabited islands. Yet once this was the seat of power in Scotland. Even when that power moved eastwards, it seemed to be no problem for the kings of Scotland to visit regularly, if for no other reason than to keep a tight rein on its allegedly turbulent inhabitants. In much later times, the burgeoning nineteenth-century middle class lived along its unpolluted shores and commuted daily to the smoke and grime of an industrialised Greenock or Glasgow. Once, people came to Argyll by boat. From Columba in his coracle to day-trippers on the *Comet*, the approach to Argyll was by water and Argyll was accessible.

The technology which in 1812 allowed the *Comet* to become the first steam-powered vessel was a godsend, a maker of fortunes, a transformer of lives. With the aid of this technology it soon became possible to commute to and from the Kyles of Bute, to travel speedily to Inverness from Glasgow via the Crinan Canal and Oban, and to deliver goods, livestock and people speedily from the islands to Glasgow. A herring caught during the night in Loch Fyne could be on a table in Glasgow in time for breakfast. Then steam technology was adapted to create railways, which scythed through previously impassable inland routes; the steam-powered engines able to haul heavy loads. Oban glittered as wealth was engendered by tourists and trade – the former arriving in style by train at its glass-roofed station to stay in luxurious new hotels, the latter shipping out on steamers to Liverpool and London. Argyll seemed set to lead the country when the first narrow-gauge line was created to carry coal from Drumlemble to Campbeltown in Kintyre. The *Campbeltown Courier* reported on 29 July 1876 that 'operations were commenced this week

An age of steam; an age of dreams. Illustration from a children's
encyclopaedia of the 1890s.

for cutting the new line of rails in connection with the Argyll Coal and
Cannel [sic] company's works at Trodigal'. Initially 4.5 miles long, it was
extended in 1881 to 4.7 miles. It was small, but it was a start, and many
believed that soon there would be railway links from the tip of Kintyre
to Oban and Dalmally.

The age of steam was an age of dreams. The children's encyclopaedia
which demonstrated the distance between the earth and the planets by
drawing railway tracks to them all with trains puffing their way along
them out into space epitomised the spirit of enterprise and imagination
– and the rash of curious plans for transport in Argyll were part and
parcel of it. An Argyll criss-crossed by tunnels, trams and trains was
on the agenda of the entrepreneurs for more than thirty years. However, the trick was to put these exciting methods of connection onto the
politicians' shopping lists and that was a much more difficult task than
drawing up intricate plans.

Any schemes to improve the infrastructure of Argyll would have been
welcomed in a rugged county 100 miles long and 80 miles wide with
over 3,000 miles of coastline. The building of the Crinan Canal and
the creation of the coastal road along Loch Fyne in the last third of the
eighteenth century had been responsible for transforming Lochgilphead

and Ardrishaig from dots on the map into prosperous junctions. The steamers turned Dunoon and Tighnabruaich from farming and fishing backwaters into fashionable resorts fringed by stately villas within a few decades. A share in such wealth was the promise implicit in engineers' drawings for tunnels, trains and tramlines.

If the entrepreneurial engineers on the Scottish side of the water were thinking that Argyll was an area in need of modern transport schemes, the Irish equally felt that if they did not have adequate links with Britain, their economy and the strained social and political relationships between the two countries could never improve. The shortest distance between Britain and Northern Ireland is, of course, the point between Kintyre and Moyle – as Columba discovered when he left his beloved Ireland behind, swearing that he would settle nowhere from whence he could still see his homeland. When he first landed at what today is known as Southend on Kintyre, making, it is said, an imprint of his footstep in the rock there, Ireland was only too clearly visible across the water.

While there may be some geological umbilical cord linking Argyll and Ireland – the Giant's Causeway and the island of Staffa are linked by legend if not by science – it is said that in AD 695 there was a natural causeway between Ballycastle and the Mull of Kintyre. The *Irish Annals of the Four Masters* record that the Sea of Moyle was frozen over that year and people were able to cross the ice with horses and carts. That winter must have been exceptional – crossings throughout the millennia have more conventionally been made with the help of a seaborne vessel. If Robert the Bruce did indeed cross to the Moyle some six centuries later, hiding out in a cave until the efforts of a spider convinced him to try his luck again against the English king, he most certainly travelled by boat. The MacDonalds – or McDonnells as they are known in Ireland – made good use of that short stretch of water. These Lords of the Isles and their followers hid out in the hills or islands of one or other territory when the situation demanded. It was on a trip to Ireland to secure more support during the British Civil Wars that Alastair MacDonald seized his Covenanting hostages, sailing with them and 1,500 Irish mercenaries to Ardnamurchan, eventually to join the Montrose forces. Some half a century later, two years after the Union of the Parliaments of England and Scotland, John McIlrevie, a sailor from Machrimore in the south of the Kintyre peninsula, paid £40 to the Dowager Duchess of Argyll for the franchise to run a ferry to Ireland, but he had to undertake not to

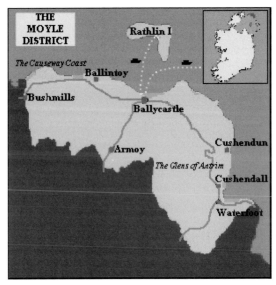

Argyll's nearest neighbours in the hills of Antrim: connected down
the centuries through the MacDonald clan and their Irish
McDonnell cousins.

transport any undesirables between the two destinations – a reflection on
traditional trafficking, which included smugglers, pedlars and beggars.

Customs officers in the eighteenth century turned a blind eye when
ferry owner James Mitchell and the master of his ferry *Eliza*, a roguish
man named James Cumming, shipped horses to Ireland without the appropriate paperwork – Mitchell and Cumming were tough characters,
according to Hugh Alexander Boyd writing for the Glens of Antrim
Historical Society. In the old days it was easier for the people of Moyle
to travel to Kintyre than to take their goods across the hills to the main
towns of Ireland. In early centuries, birlinns from Kintyre landed on
Cushendun beach. Later, a ferry ran between Dunaverty at the tip of
Kintyre and Cushendun (the name means 'the foot of the brown river'). The village of Cushendun, now a pretty tourist resort in a sheltered
harbour with a safe anchorage, grew around its ferry terminal. The seemingly ubiquitous Scottish engineer Sir John Rennie was called in around
1830 to improve the harbour and create a breakwater there, but Nicholas Cromelin, the local entrepreneur who had employed the Scot, didn't
have enough money to carry out his recommendations and the Board of
Works wouldn't finance the project.

The last ferry ran from Cushendun in 1834. By the 1870s the railway was transforming parts of the north of Ireland, as it was parts of Argyll. The Ballycastle Narrow Gauge Railway took day-trippers to the coast, farmers and their produce to market, and coal from the cliffs to the east of Ballycastle to the bigger towns. The new line, which measured 3 feet in width, was officially opened on 25 October 1880, and there were other narrow gauge lines, including Ballymena, Cushendall – a near neighbour of Cushendun – and Red Bay Railway, running through the Moyle district.

Schemes to link this corner of Ireland with Kintyre continued to be high on the agenda, and in the modern age of engineering the first plan

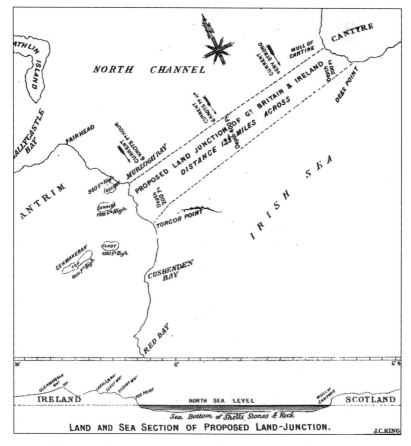

LAND AND SEA SECTION OF PROPOSED LAND-JUNCTION.

Plans were drawn up to re-create the icy causeway of the seventh century. *Glens of Antrim Historical Society.*

was to replicate that frozen causeway of AD 695. Cahal Dallat records in Volume 19 of *The Glynns*, the journal of the Glens of Antrim Historical Society, that the scheme proposed a land junction from Torr Head in County Antrim to Dees Point on the Mull of 'Cantyre'. A chart of the plan is headed 'An Isthmus to exclude the *Gulf-stream* and reclaim 1,000,000 acres of submerged land in the Irish Sea and loughs'. The land junction would have been 12.5 miles long and the landfall would have gone from a depth of around 200 feet near the coast to 400 feet at the middle of the channel. The scheme included cutting two ship canals through Kintyre, one of which would presumably have been between Crinan and Ardrishaig and the other from West to East Loch Tarbert. The first of these, the Crinan Canal, was given the green light through an Act of Parliament in 1793, and despite its many teething troubles and the fact that it was almost immediately disadvantaged by the growth in size of the new steamships, it still exists today as a major tourist attraction in Mid Argyll. A canal at Tarbert was proposed again and again, but it never became a reality. The most curious and most ambitious part of this particular scheme – to fill in the channel between Ireland and Kintyre – fortunately was rejected. What benefits such a causeway may have brought economically would most surely have been offset ecologically as the whole balance of sea and shore would have been thrown out of kilter by the massive structure. The very idea that the Gulf Stream be excluded seems a strange one today. Fishing, farming and the tourism which would become Argyll's mainstay in the future, may well have been changed irreparably. The plan was discussed in parliament but the estimated cost of £70 million and the obvious block on all shipping heading north from mainland Britain and eastern Irish ports were fortunate deterrents.

Instead, the engineers began to talk about tunnels. While tunnels were not a new idea – one was constructed for pedestrians under the River Euphrates in 2500 BC – from the early nineteenth century they began to proliferate around the world as engineering techniques and machinery improved. The first major railway tunnel in England was built between Manchester and Liverpool, opening in 1826. By the late 1860s, when it was first suggested that a tunnel between 'Cushendun and Cantyre' would be feasible, Europe was riddled with them and they were encasing railway lines in New Zealand, Canada and America. Why not run one below the 14-mile stretch of water between Ireland and Scotland? It was admitted from the outset that no amount of traffic would make such a tunnel a viable economic proposition, but politics and prestige pushed for plans to be drawn up. The world's first underwater tunnel, built under the Thames between Wapping and Rotherhithe by Marc Brunel, had opened as early as 1825. The first transalpine rail tunnel was built between 1857 and 1871 through Fréjus between France and Italy and was around 22 miles long, about the length of the tunnel for horse-drawn coaches proposed from as early as 1802 for under the English Channel. The plan for the Cushendun to Cantyre project that was formalised in 1870 was modest by comparison. At the end of the 1880s – a good decade for tunnels, when the Submarine Continental Company was set up to build a Channel tunnel, the Severn tunnel opened in 1885, and the Mersey railway tunnel in 1886 – a serious attempt was made to get a tunnel built under the Moyle channel.

The proposal was first made in 1868 by Luke Livingston Macassey, CE, and William Scott, CE, Fellow of the Royal Scottish Society of Arts. In his original report, Macassey said, 'It does not require much argument

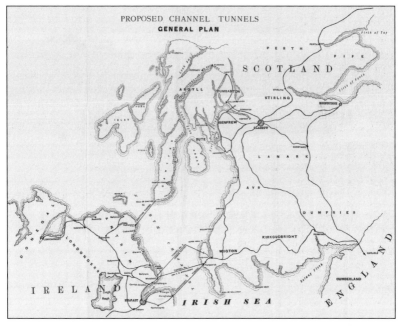

From 1868, plans for a tunnel between Antrim and Kintyre were drawn up and discussed at the highest level. *National Library of Scotland.*

to show the immense advantage resulting to Ireland by actually tying it, so to speak, to its more opulent sister.' He attributed the success of manufacturing enterprise and commerce in Belfast to its 'close connection with Scotland' and suggested that 'the world-wide reputation of both Glasgow and Belfast [would] necessarily be spread still further by their being brought nearer to one another'.

This north-eastern corner of Ireland was proving to be rich in iron ore, coal and limestone – first-class ingredients for smelting – but in the 1860s iron ore was still being imported from mother England to Ireland. Macassey saw the industrial possibilities to be created by his proposed tunnel to Kintyre: he wanted a railway line built to Helensburgh which would take in coalfields on its route. His estimate in 1870 for the tunnel and railway links from Cushendun to Ballymoney and to Larne, and from Glenstrone to Helensburgh was £4.25 million, and he saw this as a 'national work' which the Government should at least assist in paying for – a public–private partnership ahead of its time. It was his firm belief that the tunnel would bring not only national benefits, but that the close union would consolidate the British Empire, a outcome 'so greatly desired by all lovers of order and prosperity'.

For all his fervour, the plan was rejected in 1870, but Macassey was not daunted. He and others kept the idea floating and in November 1890, writing from 5 Temple Gardens, London EC, he again issued a pamphlet. In papers and maps now held by the National Library of Scotland, Macassey suggested that the public wanted such a link and that the demand for faster journey times between Ireland and Britain and on to Continental Europe made such a tunnel desirable, if not economically viable. He had revamped his arguments from the late 1860s, however. Now he wrote, 'People who were formerly satisfied to travel at the rate of twenty miles an hour are now not satisfied with anything under forty miles.' To this he added the threat of seasickness, a factor on any of the contemporary steamer routes, but particularly on the notorious stretch of water between Antrim and Kintyre. He claimed the threat made even a lengthy rail journey on the bed of the sea seem preferable. Macassey believed that 'a very large proportion of the travelling public would take advantage of the facilities thus afforded'.

In the late nineteenth century it took nine hours to reach Glasgow from Belfast via Greenock, and seven hours via the daily Larne to Stranraer route on the *Princess Victoria*. It was expected in 1890 that the planned rail link between Stranraer and Carlisle would speed up both this journey and the journey to Edinburgh, which at the time was ten and a quarter hours by Greenock and thirteen and a half via Stranraer. However, Macassey's argument was that if the whole journey was done by train via the proposed tunnel, this timetable would be slashed drastically. There were some very fanciful alternative plans being submitted at this time – a Mr Maxton, one of the members of the Belfast Natural History and Philosophical Society, put forward a proposal for a tubular bridge with its roadway running 60 feet below the surface of the sea across the 22 miles between Portpatrick and Donaghadee. The trains which would run within this steel-plated tube were to be operated by electricity or compressed air, ideas very much ahead of their time. Macassey saw them as completely impractical, and he equally dismissed the idea of a railway bridge. The Forth Railway Bridge was still a shining new example of engineering and its piers were built 'almost on dry land'. To build a comparable bridge in a channel where the water ran to depths of 600 feet it would cost around £30 million. Macassey's updated 1890 paper discusses all the alternatives in detail, pointing out that a rail tunnel from Donaghadee to Stranraer would encounter a depth of 900 feet towards the 'Scotch side', while a variation on this scheme to avoid the deep water would add considerably to the length of the tunnel.

Another tunnel had been proposed in 1889 by Messrs Barton of Dundalk [sic] which followed a 33-mile route from Island Magee in County Antrim to Wierston Hill in Wigtownshire. This one, defended hotly by Mr J. T. Barton at a meeting in Belfast on 17 October 1890, would have had a sharp bend in it, would have cost around £400,000 a mile, and would have run into difficulties because of the geological pathway it intended to follow. For several miles the tunnelling would have to be blasted through red marls which, in that area, are intersected by basaltic dykes, or whinbars, which would allow too much water into the tunnel.

Macassey was very critical of all but what he termed the 'Cantyre tunnel'. This was the most northerly – and the shortest – route and the one for which Macassey and William Scott had drawn up plans in 1868. Just 14.5 miles long, and including its approaches totalling no more than 24 miles, it was the shortest possible route and the gradients were no more difficult than one in sixty. The tunnel was to have a double line of rails and Macassey and Scott still dreamt of a new railway line running 'from the Mull of Cantyre by Campbeltown round by Inveraray, and connected to the West Highland Railway now being made, at a point south of Crianlarich'. This line would be 100 miles long, and there was also to be a new stretch of line to Larne with a connection to Londonderry.

Although he admitted that no surveying had been done on the rock which the tunnel would run through, Macassey claimed that this particular project had more in its favour than any of the others. Almost as an afterthought – despite the length of time he had been cooking up this scheme – he allowed that a 'great drawback' would be the length of connecting railways needed. He insisted, however, that travellers did not measure their journeys in miles, but by hours and by convenience – as long as they were not charged more for the privilege, of course. He cited all those passengers who chose to travel from London to Belfast via Stranraer rather than Liverpool – a journey longer by 120 miles – to save time and avoid seasickness. His table of journey times looks impressive even in the twenty-first century, taking travellers from Belfast to Edinburgh in 5.6 hours and to Glasgow in 4.6 hours by the Kintyre tunnel and the new rail line. Macassey's trump card was that whatever the cost of the extra railtrack throughout Argyll, the cost of the tunnel would be far cheaper than any of the other proposed projects. He estimated nearly £6.5 million for the tunnel and £1.1 million for the connecting lines, a mere £7.6 million in total and cheap at the price – but a jump of over £3 million in the twenty years since he and William Scott had first proposed the scheme.

The proposed tunnel through the English Channel was at this time being shouted down because of impending hostilities, but Macassey felt that no objections could be made on military grounds to the Cushendun to Cantyre tunnel. In view of the turn of affairs in Ireland in the twentieth century, Macassey's conclusion to his proposal for the Kintyre tunnel seems unrealistically optimistic. Despite the very obvious understanding that the tunnel would not 'pay a fair return on its cost', he continued to believe most strongly in its importance and advantages. This was not simply based on increased trade; he argued that 'In England and Scotland generally there is a very hazy conception of Ireland and its capacities. In fact, most Britons think of Ireland as they do of the Isle of Man, and nothing would more effectually dispel such want of knowledge as the channel tunnel, in affording a rapid and comfortable means of access to and from Ireland.'

The *Irish Builder*, a publication which described itself as 'a journal dedicated to architecture, archaeology, engineering, sanitation, arts and handicrafts', reported in Volume 32, No. 741 that at the meeting on 17 October at which both Mr Barton and Mr Macassey had rehearsed their plans for tunnels before an audience of eminent engineers, railway bosses and public figures elected and otherwise, the MP Mr W. E. Macartney had proposed a resolution in favour of a tunnel. The resolution said that bringing Antrim into 'unbroken communication with the railway systems of Scotland and Ireland would be an immense advantage to both countries' – a phrase he admitted was 'sufficiently vague' to meet with the approval of anyone in the room. It was seconded by another MP, a Colonel Waring, and passed by the assembled dignitaries under the chairmanship of the Mayor of Belfast. A committee was set up to investigate all tunnel possibilities further.

Across the water, Sir Roper Lethbridge, MP, read a paper at the Society of Arts in London on 11 February 1891 to drum up support for at least the concept of a tunnel; all the possibilities were detailed, and the Kintyre crossing was again supported as the shortest route. A vision of prosperity for all was the thrust of Lethbridge's paper and he saw no reason why the tunnel could not be constructed and maintained by a Department of State. 'I cannot imagine any form of public works of greater public utility than this tunnel', he told the Society of Arts, and he urged that a royal commission should investigate the possibilities if the government was unwilling to go ahead with the project on the current evidence.

Six years later, no progress had been made and not everyone was happy to see yet another airing of the plans. On 1 June 1897, the *Irish Builder* published a letter from a retired district surveyor named G. Henry Kinahan which referred to 'this wild scheme' again being brought before the public. The following month, the same publication reported that a joint 'Irish–English' committee had petitioned Mr Charles Thomson Ritchie – later Lord Ritchie of Dundee – for a grant of £15,000 to make borings and soundings to conclude the practicability of the tunnel to Kintyre. Ritchie, who was president of the Board of Trade from 1895 to 1900 in Lord Salisbury's government, agreed that 'anything which would make the communication between the North of Ireland and the South of Scotland more easy and simple must be desirable for many reasons'. He warned, however, that there were two important questions involved: the practicality of the tunnel and who was to pay for it. He obviously felt that the vagueness of cost estimates would be off-putting to any potential investors – and certainly to the Chancellor of the Exchequer. While Macassey had always emphasised the positive aspects of such a link, Ritchie suggested that mariners and taxpayers might not be so keen. As president of the Board of Trade, he was willing to look at more detailed plans of the tunnel and to take part in further debates, but not, at that stage, to offer up £15,000 to make borings and soundings.

This was, of course, by no means the end of it. In February 1900 Macassey's son Lynden told readers of the *Irish Builder* that the time for his father's plan for a submarine tunnel had come. The plan was now, he wrote, 'recognised as practicable'. Finance, however, was still the fly in the ointment. The younger Macassey rehearsed the different proposals, and, with tunnels to Stranraer and Portpatrick being dismissed as too long, too deep, too rocky and too steep, he pushed his father's Kintyre tunnel as the cheapest, shortest and most likely to succeed, given the proposed rail links. In the following year, Mr Barton, who of course had drawn up plans for an Ireland–Stranraer tunnel, presented a paper at the great Engineering Congress in Glasgow at which he put forward all the old plans yet again, giving estimates, diagrams and projected social and economic outcomes. By this time, Prime Minister Balfour had, according to Mr Barton, 'expressed himself desirous of seeing the project carried out' and, if the cost could be capped, willing to discuss it with his parliamentary colleagues.

Sir Douglas Fox, who had long taken an interest in the project, was at the congress in Glasgow and told delegates that while the suggestion of such a tunnel might 'takes some people's breath away', it certainly didn't frighten engineers. The chairman of these proceedings on 5 September 1901, the eminent chartered engineer Mr John Strain, said that the enormous social, political and commercial advantages of the scheme could not be overestimated. And yet, no tunnel has ever been built. While the lack of railway links went against the often-favoured shortest route for which Macassey drew plans between Cushendun and 'Cantyre', the issue of cost finally overruled the idea of any tunnel between Ireland and Scotland.

The dream had been an exciting one which had captured public imagination and engineering admiration, and the proposition to have rail links through Kintyre and on to Helensburgh was not just a figment of

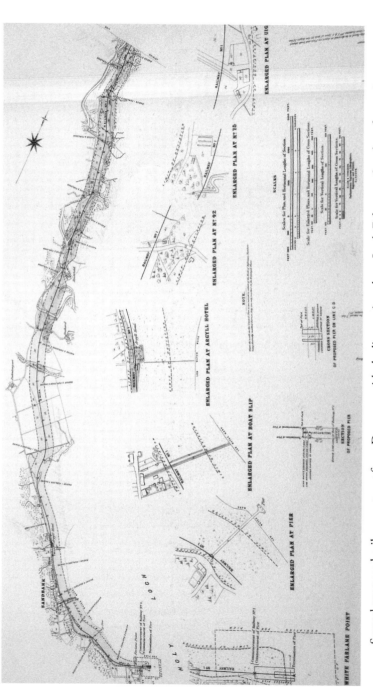

Several proposed railways set out from Dunoon, with the lines going along Loch Eck on to Strachur, from where passengers would cross Loch Fyne to Inveraray or Furnace. *Argyll and Bute Archive.*

the enthusiastic Macassey's boffin brain: plans for railways throughout Argyll proliferated from the earliest days of steam trains.

Perhaps the most concrete plan came in the late 1880s, for the Clyde, Ardrishaig and Crinan Railway; it chugged its way through parliament but, like the plans for the tunnel, hit the buffers because of lack of finance. Throughout 1887 committees at Westminster were exercised by the fine detail of this proposed railway. James Hunter of Hafton had bought up rights which included what had come to be known as Hunter's Quay on the Holy Loch. Once at Cammesreinach, the Bay of the Ferns, in the early seventeenth century, the Marquess of Argyll was able to command a ten-oared ornamental boat from there to cross the Clyde. Times had changed: Hunter's Quay had become the steamer destination of choice for thousands of Glasgow day-trippers. Now, in 1887, the Hafton Trustees, who owned the Quay, wanted the proposed railway line to start at the Holy Loch, which would shorten the line by half a mile.

Deliberation over such detail seems to have been a little premature – the desirability of such a railway was still being discussed before the Select Committee on Private Bills, and a week after the Hafton Trustees' request was looked at, evidence was heard about the pros and cons of the line. Mr Archibald Clark, a justice of the peace and a commissioner of supply for Argyll, explained to the Select Committee why he believed it would be advantageous to travel by train between Sandbank and Strachur – a ferry crossed from Strachur or St Catherine's to Inveraray, cutting off the head of the loch, which the modern road skirts round. He said that if he had to go to Inveraray from Dunoon, which borders on Sandbank, on business, it took two days to go and return if the coaches were running, and three days if they were not. The *Oban Times* of 28 May 1887 reported that Mr Clark suggested that if there was a railway 'this state of things would be very much improved'. He was not the only one to advocate the building of this line. Robert Stewart, a director of the National Bank of Scotland, was in favour of it – perhaps his shareholders were interested parties. Mr Turner, a Kintyre farmer, told the Select Committee that since he sent 1,500 sheep every year to winter in Fife, Lanark and Ayrshire, the proposed railway would be a great help to him, especially if the weather was rough when the sheep were coming back to be sold: when they travelled by boat at such times he usually to lost two or three shillings a head on the price. Mr Turner told the committee that the railway would create dairy farms in Argyllshire

– perhaps he was looking back two centuries to a time when the earls of Argyll 'planted' dairy farmers from Ayrshire on their Kintyre lands – and 'give a considerable stimulus to farming'. Even the legal profession was represented before the Select Committee, in the person of Mr George Campon, a sheriff-substitute from Inveraray, who explained that the circuit was held twice a year and that jurymen of the circuit had to come from all parts of Argyllshire, including the islands. This was particularly difficult in winter, but the proposed railway would help to bring many to within 5 miles of Inveraray.

The plans were for trains to cross Loch Fyne by a railway ferry from Newton on the north-east shore to Furnace on the west shore of the loch, south of Inverarary, and then to have a split line, with one branch going to Crinan, the other to Lochgilphead. In the engineering spirit of the age, a Mr Arrol, a mechanical engineer and contractor who had worked on the Tay and Forth bridges, told the committee that the trains could be transferred across Loch Fyne in half an hour, including the putting on and taking off, on special ferries.

When the Select Committee reconvened after the Whitsuntide holiday in 1887, more evidence in favour of the line was heard. Mr R. Graham, the agent for the Royal Bank on Islay, believed that a train link from Crinan would be of enormous benefit to the island's distillers, who had exported 1,710,000 gallons of whisky in 1886, and to the farmers who exported horses, cattle and sheep. He also believed that the fishing industry could be greatly developed if there was a railway between Crinan and Glasgow. Catches were easily transported by steamer from the east side of the peninsula, but the fishermen of Jura, Islay and Colonsay were excluded from this market – the Crinan Canal could not accommodate the larger boats of the late nineteenth century. There were, however, witnesses who said it was the tides and weather which accounted for fish not getting market from the islands, rather than lack of links from Crinan to Glasgow. Mr Douglas, a fisherman from Newton, the tiny purpose-built fishing village on the north-east bank of Loch Fyne, saw the proposed railway as a great boon in the battle against fish buyers, who were currently able to dictate prices.

Witness after witness gave their evidence over a period of many weeks, and at the beginning of July, the Select Committee passed the Clyde, Ardrishaig and Crinan Railway Bill, authorising construction of a 41-mile railway from the Holy Loch to Crinan Loch by the North British Rail-

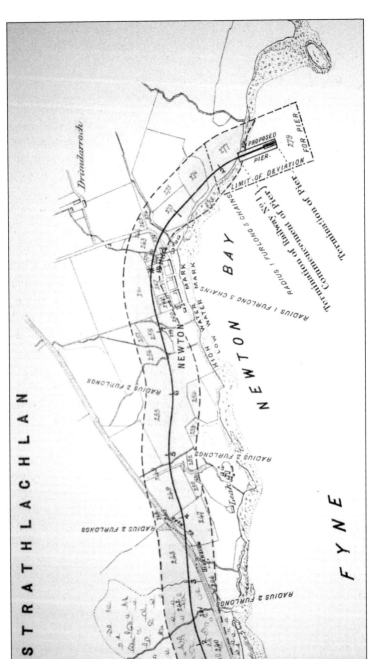

Evidence was given for and against the proposed railway lines; fishing at Newton would be well served.

Argyll and Bute Archive.

way at a cost of £141,000. It was not to be that easy, of course. By the end of July, the *Oban Times* was reporting that when the Bill went before the House of Lords Mr Gripps, a representative of the trustees for the Cumlodden Estate – site today of Crarae Gardens – proposed an alternative scheme 'which would interfere less with the estate'.

The Cumlodden Estate was the country estate of one of the cadet Campbell families. In 1887, while the railway debate rumbled on, Grace Reynell-Pack of Avsford in Sussex married Sir Archibald Campbell, 5th Baronet of Succoth. Her nephew was the traveller and plant hunter who seems to have influenced her to start the famous garden of Himalayan plants at Crarae. The family lived at Garscube – today part of Greater Glasgow – and only visited Cumlodden occasionally, but the trustees of the estate evidently did not want a railway running through the land along the western shore of Loch Fyne any more than they wanted crofters getting in the way of the development of the estate for leisure purposes. They did not always get their own way: while the Crofters Commission Report of 1893 relates that the rights of two crofters on the estate were upheld, in the issue at hand there were lots of witnesses, including Mr Forman, an engineer with the promoters of the railway, who claimed the estate would not be interfered with if the railway went ahead as planned. At the end of the day, the committee returned the Bill to the Commons with some amended clauses.

By early September, a meeting was being held in Lochgilphead by the directors of the Clyde, Crinan and Ardrishaig Railway at which Colonel Malcolm, one of the area's largest landowners and the local MP, was appointed chairman and orders were given for laying out the line. Mr Forman, of Formans and McCall, who had spoken against the changes of plan demanded by the Cumlodden Estate, was already 'on the ground', according to the *Oban Times*.

The plans drawn up for this railway in 1886 by Formans and McCall, Engineers, originally showed the railway starting at Farlane Point in Dunoon, going past the Argyll Hotel, travelling along Loch Eck to Strachur and on to Newton Bay to a terminus. The passengers – or indeed, the railway carriages containing the railway passengers – were to cross Loch Fyne here by ferry to the pier at Furnace, south of Inveraray. The railway was then to continue along Loch Fyne to Crarae, past Cumlodden Quarry, the Smithy and Whitebridge Cottages, and the track going between the cottages and the shore. From here the line was to take off west over the hills via Craig Dhu to Kilmichael Glen, past Lag, with the River Add on its right, travelling south-west to Kilmichael Glassary.

This section was, of course, the time-honoured track that has been followed for millennia by drovers and foot travellers. The railway would pass, or subsume, ancient duns and burial cairns, and, as it was marked on the plan, the 'historic Torrabhlarain' (today Torbhlaren), site of a prehistoric fort. It was to go on past Ducharnan on a line between the Add and the manse and Ballimor Farm, emerging at Bridgend. Here, this second part of the track would split to become 'Railway No. 3' and 'Railway No. 4'. The former would head to Crinan Loch across the Moine Mor, one of Scotland's most precious wetlands, and the southern end of Kilmartin Glen, now considered an area of outstanding archaeological interest. The latter would travel between Achnashelloch and Dunamuck, which was then still a substantial township. A fifth stretch of the railway was planned to run past the houses on the shore to Ardrishaig.

Argyll would have been a very different place had this line been built, although the railway would no doubt, like those in Appin and elsewhere, have been axed by the Beeching cuts of the 1960s. But, like so many plans for railways, it simply fizzled out. A decade later, North British Railways had a variation on this plan, the Loch Fyne Light Railway, which would have started at Arrochar and travelled to St Catherine's on a standard gauge track. A high embankment or a viaduct was to be built to take the line across Glen Loin from the head of Loch Long under the Cobbler, then it was to go – with some evidently very clever engineering – up Glen Croe, over the Rest and Be Thankful and down to the shore of Loch Fyne at St Catherine's, where a ferry jetty was to be built.

In 1898, suggestions were made for a route from Tarbert on Loch Fyne, at the gateway to Kintyre, to Dalmally, some 20 miles south of Oban, and this plan was revived a number of times in different guises. An Act of Parliament – yet another one – was passed in 1905 to create a railway from East to West Loch Tarbert; it had a Magnus Barefoot-like vision of taking fishing boats across the isthmus. Under a treaty with the King of Scotland which said that he could have all lands he could sail round, the Viking leader Magnus Barefoot, claimed Kintyre as his own, completing the loop by dragging a birlinn across this same narrow waist of land. In 1910, Glasgow and South Western Railway saw an opportunity in the market to link up the piers in Argyll with a rail network. The plan was to take one line south-west from Skipness, on the north-east coast of

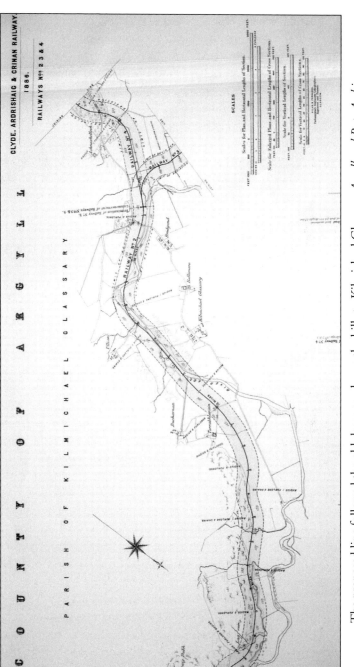

The proposed line followed the old drove road over the hills to Kilmichael Glassary. *Argyll and Bute Archive.*

the Kintyre peninsula, across Glenreasdell to Clachan, on the west coast, with a pier at Ronachan Bay to serve Islay and Jura. A second line was to travel south from a new pier at Cour Bay, south of Skipness, crossing the peninsula to Tayinloan to connect with the Gigha ferry and then running south to link with the Drumlemble line to Campbeltown. Another line was planned to go to Southend, with a pier at Dunaverty to meet a ferry to Ireland.

Then there was the plan to make links throughout Argyll from either the Caledonian line at Dalmally or from the North British line at Arrochar, along the lines of the links proposed by L. L. Macassey to make his tunnel viable. Some landlords were enthusiastic – J. R. Moreton of Largie liked the idea of a Campbeltown–Tarbert link enough to offer a 6-mile stretch across his land free of charge, and his neighbour, P. J. Mackie of Glenreasdell, thought that the line was a good use for surplus government rails from France and gave 10 miles across his estate.

By now, these unrealised plans were two a penny and yet another curious project which never left the starting blocks was dreamt up in 1919, to link Arrochar and Glenkinglas with a light gauge railway fed through a 1.5-mile tunnel through the Rest and Be Thankful. At the time, road traffic was beginning to increase, but the technology did not exist to upgrade the tortuous road through Glen Croe which had been built in the eighteenth century by General Wade to aid troop movement and help quell rebellious Highlanders.

Curiously, despite all these innovative plans, the combined forces of Victorian engineering skills, redundant train-ferries looking for a home after the building of the Forth Rail Bridge, the Light Railways Act of 1897, and the surplus railway sleepers brought home from France after the First World War could not bring a railway system into being in south-west Argyll. Some of the ideas which were floated seem as curious as the image of a train going to the moon, yet the projects for tunnels, viaducts and train-ferries seem rational when set against Daniel Anderson's plans for a tram system throughout Argyll – a system which he believed would solve all the county's transport problems.

A pamphlet entitled 'Argyllshire's Needs and How to Meet Them' was produced in 1910 by Mr Anderson, a former solicitor from Dunoon, sometime honorary sheriff-substitute and county council member for Argyll among other distinguished posts. Mr Anderson had suffered an illness in 1909 and was confined to bed in Oxford, where he passed his time musing on the problems of Argyll's transport system. He considered the old trade routes from Oban to Loch Awe, the ferry across Loch Awe to Port Sonachan, the road thence to Inveraray, the ferry to St Catherine's, the road to Dunoon and the ferry to Cloch on the other side of the Clyde which took travellers from the west on into the 'mainland' of Scotland.

This was a route which had been followed for centuries by drovers and chapmen, kings and councillors. It had been followed because it was carved out by nature. It worked. Mr Anderson also mused on the growing monopolies being created by steamboat and railway companies, which were squeezing out other forms of transport, including the small ferries which had operated in some form or other for at least a thousand years. The monopolies, coupled with an overzealous Board of Trade which operated its regulations with an iron hand, were leaving Argyll behind in the transport stakes: so many of the new schemes had fallen at the last hurdle because of lack of finance or stringent regulations; so many old links were being cut because of the power wielded by the major transport companies.

Lying in his sick bed, Mr Anderson cast his mind across the Atlantic and came up with a tramway system throughout Argyll. This may have been inspired by the light reading in which he indulged during this period of incapacity – 'The Development of the Trolley in America' by George Ethelbert Walsh, an article which had been published in *Cassier's Magazine* in February of 1909; 'Power From The Farm Brook' by Donald Cameron Shafer, from the *American Review of Reviews* of January 1909; and 'Train Ferries', published in *The Engineer* in its 6 September 1907 issue. He also read the 16 and 30 July 1909 editions of *Engineering* and various reports in the *Glasgow Herald* and *Newcastle Chronicle*, and from these he pieced together his master plan.

He learned that in America tramway lines were criss-crossing the country like 'a spider's web'. The trams in America were allowed to carry heavy freight and animals, and not only were the fares cheap, so were the gas and electricity by which the trams were powered. In Newcastle, Swan, Hunter and Co. had launched a train-ferry in 1909 which carried a complete train of eight bogie vehicles back and forth across the Baltic Sea, providing a short cut from Stockholm to Berlin. This ferry train also had 'luxurious' sleeping accommodation for 96 first-class and 45 third-class passengers – railways seemed to see second class as unlucky and it was therefore omitted, like the thirteenth floors of hotels. Such ferries were beginning to proliferate, and Anderson began to visualise a system of trams traversing Argyll, linked across its many sea and freshwater lochs by similar vessels. Once his interest was aroused and his health restored, Anderson watched

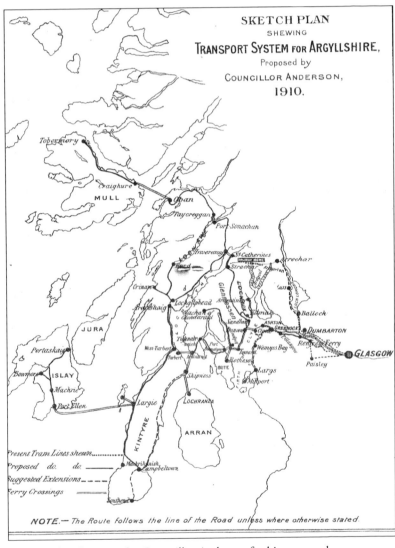

Plan drawn up by Councillor Anderson for his proposed tram system in Argyll. *Argyll and Bute Archive.*

trials on the Clyde of a train-ferry built by Inglis of Pointhouse for service on the River Plate.

Another such train-ferry was rumoured to be under construction for a New York to Cuba run, which impressed Anderson so much that he wrote, 'One may board the train in New York and be taken IN THE SAME CARRIAGE [Anderson's capitals] to Santiago de Cuba in about 40 hours.' What the implications of such a train-ferry would have been, in view of the political relationship between Cuba and the United States for the past half century, is very interesting indeed. Still another such train-ferry was contracted for operation between the islands on the eastern seaboard of Canada, and an extension was planned to take passengers and freight on to America. Anderson also learned that there were train-ferries in operation or planned for the Straits of Messina, between Germany and Denmark, and for the Great Lakes bordering Canada and the United States.

What was good enough for the Baltic, the Straits of Messina, New-foundland *et al.* was, in Anderson's view, good enough for Argyll. His research convinced him that the train-ferry was well enough established to warrant a system of tramways and tram-ferries 'not only applicable to town and country districts, but equally suitable for the crossing of such narrow rivers as the Clyde (at Glasgow) and . . . the broader waters of Argyll'. His idea was to replace contemporary means of transport with tramways and tram-ferries from Oban via Loch Awe, Loch Fyne and the Firth of Clyde to Cloch. From Cloch, there would be connections with Port Glasgow, Greenock and Gourock tramway system. He planned to replace the Erskine ferry with a tram-ferry and with tramways connecting with the Dumbarton and Loch Lomond system and with the tram system running in Glasgow on the north side of the Clyde. The Renfrew ferry was also to be converted into a tram-ferry.

Trams were by this time an accepted and efficient means of urban transport. Anderson's curious vision for the system was to make it work in the hills and across the waters of Argyll. Following similar plans to those envisaged by earlier railway enthusiasts, tramlines would run from Dunoon to St Catherine's via Glen Masson, and from Garrachra Glen and Balliemeanoch to Strachur. There would be a local branch line from Dunoon and Sandbank to Ardentinny and a line from Inveraray to Loch-gilphead, Ardrishaig and West Tarbert, with branches from Lochgilphead to Loch Awe and Crinan and from West Tarbert to Tarbert. Anderson

identified routes which would avoid steep gradients, and that meant
looking to the west side of Kintyre to take a tramline down to Campbeltown. He also envisaged a tram-ferry from Largie to Port Ellen on Islay,
a distance of some 20 miles.

This was just the start of his grand scheme. Dunoon and Rothesay,
both of which already had their own tram systems, would be linked
and tram-ferries would run to Tighnabruaich and Millport on Cumbrae.
Ardyne Point would be linked by tramway along the east side of Loch
Striven and through Glen Striven, Ardtarig and Balliemor to Glendaruel.
Anderson said, 'By such a system all the populous places in the county
would be linked together, and it would be comparatively simple to get
from or to any part of the county.' He drew a complex map, but he also
had thought for the comfort of passengers, stipulating that there should
be 'through cars' which gave the option of remaining in the tramcar or
moving about the steamer while crossing the ferries.

Anderson was thorough in his proposals for such a system. His ambitious concept was that mail, fish, agricultural produce, timber, peat,
livestock, game, wool, whisky, stone and slate from the quarries at Clu-
niter (Innellan), Bullwood (Dunoon), Crarae, Easdale, Ballachuilish and
Bonawe, and aluminium from the works at Kinlochleven would all be
exported on the tram-ferries. Imports to Argyll on the system would
include mail, newspapers, livestock, agricultural requirements, house-
building materials, yachts, fishing and motor boats, furniture, stage
properties and all sorts of merchandise. All of these commodities would
obviously be transported within the county, too. Anderson was a man
who did his homework and he came up with the fact that the Cowal
district alone – one of seven districts within Argyll – set aside £775 for
the freight of road metal in 1910, an estimate which did not include the
roads within the burgh of Dunoon. His point was that this proposed
transport system would have a guaranteed list of clients. He added to this
list of freight the seasonal passengers who would travel to Argyll between
June and September. He envisaged farmers loading sheep onto tramcars
at their own farms or at convenient nearby stations which would then be
delivered direct to the salesmen's stances in the Glasgow cattle market or
the wintering farms of Ayr, Renfrew, Lanark and Dumbarton. He saw
coals being delivered from the pithead to the steading, rather than several means of transport being loaded and unloaded. In Anderson's day,
this still included the puffer pulling onto Argyll beaches to deliver coal,

which then had to be loaded again onto carts. He imagined the golfer getting on a tram in St Vincent Place in Glasgow and arriving via tram-ferry in Machrihanish in time for a round before lunch. His grand plan took in the tourist getting on board the *Columba* at the Broomielaw in Glasgow, sailing to Oban via the Crinan Canal, taking a 'toosie tea at the Tram Hotel in Oban' and catching the 6 o'clock express by the No. 3 tram-ferry route across Loch Awe, Loch Fyne and the Clyde to Glasgow's St Enoch Square – all in time for supper by his own fireside.

This tram-ferry miracle would, according to Anderson, bring Argyll residents 'within the pale of civilisation' by enabling them to discuss the newspapers with their breakfast every morning. His concession to the Argyll terrain was that while trams in America travelled at 60 miles per hour, those in Argyll would be able to go no faster than 30 mph. The advantages he foresaw went further than a newspaper with the tea and marmalade: shorter sea routes, a time saving, and comfortable land routes was the deal offered to passengers. The authorities would benefit because they would not have to build piers – one would do a whole district – nor erect and maintain roadmen's houses in isolated areas. The construction and maintenance of roads would be less costly, waterpower could be used, there would be benefits for industry, increased employment, and better transport for school children, and the system could be extended to Ireland – no need for tunnels when a tram-ferry could link the two countries.

Legislation at the time meant that this was not a plan which the local authority could put into operation: it would have to go before parliament. Anderson wanted the county and town councils of Argyll to make representation to the government, but if the response was unfavourable, he was able to advise that under Section 17 of the Tramway Act of 1870, if two or more local authorities made joint application for the power to construct tramways, they could get round government negativity.

It was such a peerless plan, taking the tram from the heart of the city to the depths of rural Argyll. It was, like the rest of these curious transport plans, never to see the light of day. Only the Drumlemble line actually had its glory days, when thousands of tons of coal and thousands of day-trippers were transported by the 'wee train', advertised throughout the UK as the Atlantic Express and puffing its Toy Town way from Campbeltown to Machrihanish's silver sands. But such curious ideas did not disappear with the heady days of Victorian and Edwardian

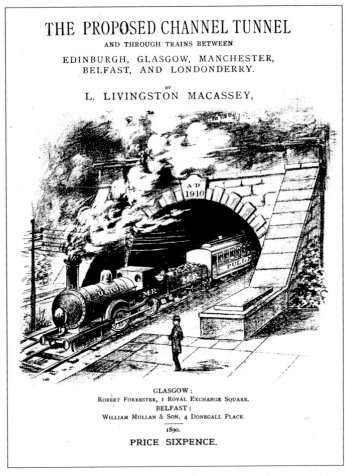

THE PROPOSED CHANNEL TUNNEL
AND THROUGH TRAINS BETWEEN
EDINBURGH, GLASGOW, MANCHESTER,
BELFAST, AND LONDONDERRY.

BY

L. LIVINGSTON MACASSEY,

A·D
1910

GLASGOW:
ROBERT FORRESTER, 1 ROYAL EXCHANGE SQUARE.
BELFAST:
WILLIAM MULLAN & SON, 4 DONEGALL PLACE.

1890.

PRICE SIXPENCE.

Tunnels, trains and trams were on the agenda into the twentieth
century. Intricate plans and arguments were presented in this 1890s
pamphlet for the Antrim–Kintyre tunnel. *National Library of Scotland.*

engineering genius. Come 1969 one A. Robert Powell, a chartered civil
engineer with special experience of studying traffic needs, entered the
field. In a booklet entitled 'The Moine Mhor and Beyond', Mr Powell,
who hailed from Law in Lanarkshire, proposed a 29-mile-long motorway from Inverkip in Renfrewshire to West Otter Ferry on Loch Fyne,
involving major bridge and tunnel crossings of the Firth of Clyde and
Loch Fyne and minor crossings of the Eachaig River, Glen Tarsan Burn,
Glen Laoigh and the River Ruel. The purpose of this super highway

was to serve a new town the size of East Kilbride – what the *Argyllshire Advertiser* of Tuesday, 16 September 1969 described as 'a huge industrial settlement – a kind of Grangemouth, Invergordon and Ravenscraig rolled into one'.

Mr Powell saw the Moine Mhor – valued by others as one of Scotland's most precious wetlands – as the ideal site for three oil refineries, a power station and a steelworks, and thought that it would 'still have sufficient room for an international airport with runways at least two miles long and a township the size of East Kilbride on its fringes'. This, he said, would enhance the prosperity of the Highlands and offer work for skilled resources from the Lowlands. The motorway was to by-pass Lochgilphead and go beyond by way of Cairnbaan, Island Add Bridge and Duntrune Castle.

The proposal, which would have destroyed huge swathes of Argyll's natural beauty, historical heritage and archaeological legacy, was perhaps not made with the same serious intent as the plans of Macassey, Anderson & Co. Mr Powell submitted his booklet to William Ross, Secretary of State for Scotland, as his objection to the multimillion-pound proposal by the South of Scotland Electricity Board for an oil-fired power station at Inverkip. His proposal, then, had much more to do with the heavy irony of protest than the zeal of engineering inventiveness. Fortunately, Willie Ross did not pursue the idea; unfortunately, southern Argyll still has no transport links with Ireland.

5

FAMILY FOLLIES

The most obvious curiosity in Oban is the Colosseum-style building which dominates the townscape. It has been called the Crown of Oban, is signposted as McCaig's Tower, but is referred to as McCaig's Folly. The Collins *English Dictionary* defines a folly as 'a building in the form of a castle, temple, etc., built to satisfy a fancy or conceit, often of an eccentric kind'. John Stuart McCaig of Muckairn and Soroba may have had some eccentricities, and there may even possibly have been some conceit in the fact that he not only placed a plaque on the building which reads 'Erected in 1900 by John Stuart McCaig, art critic and philosophical essayist and banker, Oban', but also left instructions in his will to have bronze statues of the McCaig family placed around the tower; but he did not create this incongruous edifice on a mere whim. In fact, he could have added 'philanthropist' to his plaque, because this massive undertaking on its very difficult site was begun to give unemployed Oban stonemasons a job.

The tower is iconic: a beacon for homecomers and visitors alike. Its shape, said to have been inspired by McCaig's visit to Italy in the winter of 1880–81, echoes Oban's semicircular bay. The circular screen wall is punctuated by two tiers of pointed Gothic-style apertures which in the century or so since the tower was finished have framed myriad photographs and sketches of the panorama which lies below, into which are gathered the islands of Kerrera, Mull and Lismore. Had the building existed in the 1850s during the Crimean War, when the 3rd Argyllshire Artillery Volunteers were posted on Battery Hill, the whole nation would have felt secure behind its bulk. McCaig, however, did not buy the land until 1875, by which time, although the heavy guns were still in place, the regiment had moved its headquarters from Oban to Campbeltown on the orders of the Duke of Argyll as lord-lieutenant of the county. The guns were still sitting on Battery Hill two decades later, in July of 1895, when McCaig at last applied for a building warrant to erect a semicircular

The tower built by John Stuart McCaig still dominates the
Oban skyline.

stone lime wall behind the battery. The following year, with the building already well in hand, McCaig made another application, this time
to build a full circle. In 1897 he asked for permission to increase the
height of the walls by 15 feet. The masons worked on the project when
they had no other employment, and in 1900 it was complete. There had
been an ambitious plan to add a 95-foot-high central tower that would
have included a museum, art gallery and chapel. Perhaps by 1900 the
77-year-old McCaig was running out of steam. His death two years later
gave ownership of the building – and indeed his estate – to his sister
Catherine, who preferred to put funds in the direction of Oban's poor
rather than further elaborating the tower her brother had created. Perhaps Catherine saw it as a 'folly', although the income it had provided
for men who would otherwise have found it hard to support their families when the building trade was idle was as generous and as practical as
the money which she left for the sustenance of the poor of Oban after
her death in 1913.

On the face of it, she had far more reason to accuse another of her
brothers of folly, for it was the proposition of the Rev. Donald McCaig
to bring the University of St Andrews to Oban and set it up in the massive building first intended as a hydropathic hotel. This building was
clearly visible from Battery Hill, sitting as it did at the same dizzy level
above the town, just a few hundred yards to the south.

Before we look in more detail at this seemingly foolish suggestion, a bit of context is necessary. Ironically, at this time Oban boasted, per capita, more hotels than Edinburgh, while crofters throughout Argyll and the Highlands and Islands were about to be the subject of a national inquiry into the state of their poverty and hardship. Perhaps it was because the McCaigs came from a farming family and knew the difficulties of life on a low income that all eight members of that generation invested so much in the welfare of those less well off than themselves.

The McCaigs, four brothers and four sisters, the surviving children of Malcolm McCaig and Margaret Stewart, were born on the island of Lismore. Malcolm McCaig was a merchant and farmer who died in 1834, leaving Margaret to carry on farming for another decade. There was only a small living to be had on the island and the two oldest went off to Oban to work. In an age of instant gratification, it is hard to believe that simple hard work made the McCaig fortunes. There are distant descendants of the extended family – all eight died unmarried – who believe that a find of sapphires from a Spanish galleon was the source of their wealth. Indeed, if we were to attribute all Oban's success stories to wrecks conveniently offering up treasure, then we would have to assume that the Stevensons, fathers of the town, were also lucky.

These two brothers, John and Hugh, moved to Oban from Appin in the early eighteenth century when their mother was widowed. She

A sadly faded photograph of the McCaig family; born in Lismore, all eight contributed to the welfare of the people of Oban. *Argyll and Bute Archive.*

was able to make just enough of a living to send her boys to school. Hugh was then apprenticed as a mason and lived at Glencruitten Farm. He soon opened a shop selling spirits, which was no doubt very profitable, while John trained as a joiner and took Glenshellach Farm. These two glens, Cruitten and Shellach, sculpt today's Oban. The two brothers used their skills in building boats, some as big as 80 tons. As Oban developed as a seaport, they rented out boats; as the population grew, they turned to house building. Luck seems to have little to do with it, and perhaps it is more true to say that there is something in the Oban air which encourages entrepreneurship. In the next century, the McCaigs followed the Stevensons in turning their hands as they could, making fortunes, eventually emulating them in buying the Soroba Estate.

All eight McCaigs worked hard for their fortune. Duncan was the oldest of the family, born in 1822. When he left Lismore, he set himself up in Oban as a draper, and by 1841 the census was showing that he and John Stuart, a year his junior, were living together in what was then George Street, later to become John Street. John worked as Duncan's assistant and then, as the business developed, went into partnership with him. Duncan joined the 3rd Argyllshire Artillery Volunteers and henceforth was known by the courtesy title of 'the Major'. Both Duncan and John had the Stevenson touch and spread their business wings in many directions. In 1848 a gas-works was built – although there was no street lighting until 1863 – and John became chairman and principal shareholder of the Oban Gas Company. In the 1860s, D & J McCaig's Tobacco Manufactory was founded in Breadalbane Street, and the brothers later leased the business to Blacks the tobacconists. Duncan and John also became agents for the North of Scotland Bank. John then bought the North Pier in 1873, profiting from the booming tourism industry, and he took a second bite at the cherry by selling the pier for £16,500 in 1896.

Brother Dougald, who was born in 1824, started his career as an Inland Revenue officer and later became a general merchant in the town. Donald, the youngest son, was born in 1825. He was educated in the island of Lismore, before going to Oban Burgh School – then situated where the Callander–Oban goods station was later built – and was seen even then as a young person with a richly endowed mind and a broad imagination. He was very young when he went up to Glasgow University, where he distinguished himself in moral philosophy, coming second in the list of honours. He did a course of theological study at the Free Church College of Edinburgh, but decided not to remain within that church. Instead he matriculated at St Andrews University and spent several years at Divinity Hall – where he came first in two out of his four classes – before being licensed to preach by the Presbytery of Lorn in May 1854. His first charge was as an assistant to the Rev. Dr Norman MacLeod of St Columba's Church of Scotland in Glasgow. Here the Church held him in such high esteem that a procedural point was stretched, and, although he was still only an assistant, he was ordained on 22 May 1855.

Meanwhile, the McCaig daughters were also making their way in life. Jane and Anne were in business together as dressmakers. Catherine and Margaret seem to have looked after the family estate once the older brothers had bought the lands of Soroba and Muckairn as their businesses expanded. Catherine, as we have seen, inherited from John and left funds for the poor, while Margaret left her moveable estate to the United Free Church in Oban.

Every member of this remarkable family contributed to the common good of Oban in some way, but the two men who were involved in Oban's most curious buildings perhaps gave most of themselves. John, of tower fame, became a town councillor, and he was appointed, among other civic posts, Inspector of the Poor and Chief Magistrate of the Burgh – the equivalent of provost or mayor. Donald was greatly influenced by Dr MacLeod, father of one of the leading campaigners for the rights of crofters and a man who gave great practical help to those whose sad destination was the city during the Clearances.

The Duke of Argyll had been no less guilty of evicting crofting tenants than many landowners – in the 1840s and 50s he had 'pruned' tenants from Tiree. Few, however, were as brutal as Patrick Sellar, the Sutherland land factor who moved into northern Argyll and evicted those whose stories the Rev. Norman MacLeod was to relate to the Napier Commission, which was set up by the Government in 1883 to investigate the plight of Scotland's crofters.

The commission was headed by Lord Napier, a former governor of Madras, and throughout the whole land reform controversy the crofters' situation was compared to land reform for subsistence farmers in India or Egypt, or to the emancipation of Russian peasants. Henry George, an American economist and land reformer who toured the Highlands and

Muckairn Church, Taynuilt, where Rev. Donald McCaig was minister from 1859. *Crown copyright © Royal Commission on the Ancient and Historical Monuments of Scotland.*

Islands at the time of the commission, reported that more than a third of Scottish families lived in not more than one room and more than two-thirds in not more than two rooms 'while thousands of acres are kept as playgrounds for strangers'. The situation became particularly brutal when crofters in Skye revolted in April 1882 and police from Glasgow and military troops were brought in to quell the Battle of the Braes. Rent strikes and land raids spread and the editor of the *Oban Times*, a 21-year-old firebrand called Duncan Cameron, wrote many passionate editorials in their support. The Napier Report came out in 1884 and in the 1885 general election, the Rev. Donald McCaig threw his hat into the electoral ring in support of the crofters.

By this time, he had served for a year as parish minister in Watten, a village in Caithness between Wick and Thurso, before transferring to the parish of Muckairn in 1859. Here, in a parish centred around Taynuilt, which had existed in the annals since the thirteenth century, Donald McCaig had made his support for the crofters very clear in many ways.

Coming from Lismore, he knew that the south-western end of that island had been cleared completely from the 1840s, when there had been a population of nearly four hundred people. This land had been owned by John Campbell of Combie, who, like so many traditional lairds, had been forced to sell up. It was bought by William Cheyne, who had an estate in Fife, of whom Duncan MacDonald, a Lismore boat-builder, told the Napier Commission, 'First he impoverished us, then he sent us away – one by one until he had the land all to himself.' Margaret – or Peggy – McCaig had been one of those to leave in the mid 1840s, taking the remaining six youngsters with her to Oban to join her older sons Duncan and John. Donald McCaig was also aware of clearances in the far north of Scotland from his brief stay at Watten, and in Taynuilt he was a leader of a zealous branch of the Highland Land Law Reform Association.

It was said in his obituary in the *Oban Times* that his 'works of charity and benevolence were well known'. He had spoken out loudly against all instances of oppression and for the cause of the crofter, the small farmer and the cottar. When he declared himself a candidate for parliament he boldly declared: 'Those who till the land should own it.' However, the *Oban Times*' editor was a stickler for correctness, and, despite his support of the cause, he could not countenance a minister of the Church of Scotland standing for parliament without first having severed his connections with the Church. It was, declared the paper's leader column, against the law in 1885 for a man of the cloth to stand as an MP, and so Donald's brother John took on the mantle as a candidate for Westminster. At the end of the day, D. H. Macfarlane was returned for the Crofters' Party of Argyll with 3,340 votes to 2,856 for the Liberal candidate, and 670 for John Stuart McCaig, supporting the crofters on a Liberal ticket.

Donald McCaig also worked ardently for the crofters in many ways other than political, however. He wanted status for the Highlands and Islands, and like Professor John Stuart Blackie, one of Scotland's most famous Victorian academics, whose retreat was at Altnacraig, a house near the old carding mill on the south-eastern outskirts of Oban, Donald believed that a Gaelic church and a Celtic university would bring that status. Professor Blackie had advocated a Celtic Chair at Edinburgh University from the 1870s – and was largely instrumental in achieving that foundation. Mr McCaig was on a different tack, and it was this which led to his most curious suggestion. This was a man who from his earliest days in the ministry had worked with those who were forced not only to seek the bread which their lairds had torn from their hands, but who also found it hard to gain further education because of their location and the fact that Gaelic was their native tongue.

As minister of Muckairn Parish on one of his brother John's estates – the other was Soroba, bought in 1883 – he was not a conventional man. According to a history of the parish, he didn't keep records, never went to Presbytery meetings and certainly did not attend General Assemblies. Yet his passion for the Highland cause took him for the first, and last, time to the General Assembly of the Church of Scotland in 1883. It had been agreed at a meeting of the Lorn Presbytery in May of that year that McCaig would present a motion at the assembly proposing the erection of a Celtic or Caledonian Church in the Highlands according to the Presbyterian form of church government and the Confession of Faith 'as being necessary to the temporal as well as spiritual interests of the Highlands'.

This was not the way it turned out. One of the main issues debated by the General Assembly in 1883 was the Universities (Scotland) Bill. The Church of Scotland was greatly distressed by Clause VII of the Bill, which suggested that theological professors would no longer be required to make 'any acknowledgement or declaration of religious creed' – a requirement which had been in place since an Act of Queen Anne in 1707 secured the Protestant religion and Presbyterian Church

The Rev. Donald McCaig of Muckairn caused a stir at the 1883 General Assembly of the Church of Scotland. *Muckairn Parish Collection.*

government. When the assembly met on 30 May in Edinburgh, seven motions were heard. The general feeling to emerge about Clause VII was that there should be a petition drawn up by the assembly to object to a proposal which – in the words of the second motion – could 'permit the introduction into the theological chairs of professors who may teach whatsoever doctrines they please', and could result in teaching that 'may be destructive of the religious principles entertained and professed by the Church of Scotland and other Protestant Churches of this country'. The debate ran over to Friday, 1 June, when a sixth motion suggested that this clause was 'calculated to unsettle the relations of Church and State in Scotland'.

It was then that Donald McCaig intervened with a seventh motion. Extraordinarily, it went off on a completely different tack from the previous motions, proposing 'That the Assembly petition the Government to have the University of St Andrews transferred to Oban or some other central and convenient place in the Highlands for promoting the interests of education, religion and commerce in that interesting and important part of Her Majesty's dominion, and to have it properly equipped and endowed for the purpose.'

Perhaps not surprisingly, this motion was not seconded and a vote went in favour of the motion which had been presented by Dr William Milligan, Professor of Divinity and Biblical Criticism at the University of Aberdeen. A committee was appointed to draw up an appropriate petition to deliver to the government.

But Donald McCaig's motion – and a number of other interventions made during the course of the assembly which displayed his rapier wit and stinging sarcasm – made him the star of the week. There were reports not only in the local press but in the *Evening Express*, where the newspaper's correspondent himself employed some heavy irony, describing McCaig as having 'burst upon the General Assembly of the Church of Scotland like a meteor from the midnight sky, and . . . enlightened it upon many subjects'. The idea of the Highlands being the location of a seat of learning was evidently a step too far for this sophisticated city journalist, who nonetheless appreciated Mr McCaig having given the assembly 'a number of pleasant half hours'. The *Oban Times*, on the other hand, took McCaig's suggestions – and his part in the proceedings – seriously and reminded the city slickers that Mr McCaig had been a much-lauded student at three universities himself.

In fact, although Mr McCaig had spiked his guns by bringing up the issue in the middle of the debate which aimed to preserve the sanctity and hegemony of the Presbyterian Church in Scotland, his suggestion was not as incongruous as it may appear at first glance. Within the same Universities (Scotland) Bill, Clause VIII proposed to give the government's commissioners the power to dissolve the ancient University of St Andrews because of its lack of funding, and indeed, on 4 June 1883, it was agreed by the assembly that another petition be drawn up against this. St Andrews, where McCaig had himself studied, had been in trouble for a decade. In the 1870s the student population was fewer than 150, but perhaps more pertinent was the fact that there was a chronic lack of endowments to keep the place going. By 1882 the average number of students at Aberdeen was 813, at Glasgow it was 2,320 and at Edinburgh, 3,340. St Andrews had just 193 students. The annual amounts paid by the government to Scottish universities were £7,705 for Glasgow, £7,187 for Aberdeen, and £9,393 for Edinburgh. St Andrews received just £4,036.

It is hard to know at this distance whether McCaig's proposal to move the university, lock, stock and barrel, to Oban or elsewhere in the Highlands was simply opportunist, transferring the want of a Celtic Church, which he had been commissioned to propose by Lorn Presbytery, to the want of a university. It would not have been a popular move: the idea of losing Scotland's oldest surviving seat of learning was wounding to the pride and affections not only of alumni but of the nation as a whole. Eighteen months later, when the positive future of the university was almost settled, Donald James Mackay, 11th Lord Reay, elected as rector of St Andrews from 1884–86, was stirringly supportive in his Rectorial Address on 30 January 1885, telling his audience, 'The idea of closing the annals of this University is repugnant to all classes of our countrymen.'

Perhaps McCaig did not want his alma mater closed, and it is perhaps irreverent and disrespectful to suggest that he would have sold his soul to see St Andrews moved to Oban, but his passion for the idea was great enough to risk the amusement of his peers at the General Assembly. What those peers did not perhaps know when McCaig picked up his hat and cane and left the Assembly over a point of order was that the locus for the university was ready-built: as he later explained, the bankrupt hydropathic was an ideal site.

By the late nineteenth century, Oban was growing as a tourist
resort and was an ideal spot for a fashionable hydropathic hotel.
A. Stanley, *c.* 1857. *Crown copyright © Royal Commission on the
Ancient and Historical Monuments of Scotland.*

McCaig's proposed university was to be housed within the folly of
investors who had overstepped their mark. Three main factors had created a very healthy tourism industry in Oban. The *Comet* was launched
in 1812 and was the forerunner of generations of steamers which would
deliver hordes of passengers to Oban. Before the railways, the quick-
est route from Glasgow to Inverness was by sea, via the Crinan Canal,
Oban, Fort William and the Caledonian Canal. Many stayed at Oban,
enchanted in the first instance by its natural beauty and then by the
high-class hotels which rapidly went up in the second half of the nineteenth century. In 1847, Queen Victoria and Prince Albert docked in
Oban on their Highland Tour and were highly complimentary about the
town, cementing its place on the tourist schedule. Then travel was made
so much easier for those tourists when the railway reached Oban in June
1880. Within months of this momentous event a group of investors
were planning the erection of a hydropathic hotel in the town.

In the fifth monthly report of the company's early history, covering 1868 to 1919, Sir Robert McAlpine and Sons, one of the major
companies contracted to build the hotel, chart the sorry course of that
hydropathic. Some idea of the scale of the building is given in the fact
that this was to be the largest building undertaken by the company,

which had previously erected the massive Singer factories at Kilbowie near Clydebank. The hydropathic movement originated in Austria in the 1830s, according to Dr Alastair Durie, formerly of the Department of Economic and Social History at Glasgow University. It soon spread to Britain and became particularly popular in Scotland, where by the mid 1880s there were eighteen hydropathic hotels or spas. The Oban venture was to have been one of the most ambitious. As the name implies, this was a system of water treatments for a range of ailments. Patients – self-indulgent, with disposable income and perhaps suffering more from hypochondria than anything else – were treated over a period of weeks; hence the luxurious hotel buildings with rooms for visitors, pets and servants. Billiard and music rooms inside and golf courses and walkways outside were part of the experience. A resident doctor supervised the treatments, which involved cold-water baths, showers and sessions wrapped in wet sheets and blankets. The rigours of such treatments were supported by plain food, exercise and conversation. Alcohol was not an approved part of the regime, though Dr Durie suggests that there may have been some patients who added the water to a dram, and in Oban, the proposed hydropathic had a good view down onto the local distillery.

Some of the hydro hotels in Scotland could take up to three hundred guests. With success stories at Seamill on the Ayrshire coast, Clunie in Forres, Crieff, Bridge of Allan and a dozen more, it was no wonder that investors were looking for additional appropriate sites. Even the huge building costs and operating seasons cut short by the Scottish weather did not deter the companies, each bent on bringing big profits to their shareholders. Indeed, 'hydropathic mania' seems to have swept Scotland from the 1870s. When the Oban Distillery building was put up for sale in the *Glasgow Herald* in June 1871, it advertised itself as being 'from its position, its frontage, [and] a right of water . . . specially adapted for a large Hotel or Hydropathic Establishment'. Through the decade, hydropathics were built at Waverley, near Melrose, at Kilmacolm, and at Peebles, for sums ranging between £20,000 and £80,000.

In 1880, the arrival of the railway in Oban presaged the formation of the Oban Hills Company with a capital of £70,000 and there was a spate of publicity throughout Britain in publications as diverse as the *London Figaro* and the *Banffshire Journal*. Despite this, the response was poor and the company had to scale down the project. The original plans must have been particularly extravagant: the building which went ahead was the size of a showy medieval castle. It was designed by the architect J. Ford-Mackenzie, who described himself as an 'ardent hydrotherapist' with practical knowledge of such establishments, and, in 1881, tenders were sought and had to be lodged not later than 12 noon on Monday, 2 May. Scottish baronial in style, it featured turrets and towers; there were to be cultivated grounds; water was to be pumped from the sea; and all was to be made for a sum 'not exceeding £32,000 to £33,000', according to Dr Robert Orr of Glasgow, who was in the chair at an extraordinary general meeting of the Oban Hills Company on 17 May 1881. This was to be a middle-of-the-road project able to compete with other 'magnificent establishments' but not in the league of Pitlochry hydropathic, which had cost £100,000 to build.

Ambitiously, the company wanted this up and running by the summer season of 1882, with 137 guest bedrooms and numerous servants' bedrooms. There were to be several private parlours, a large dining room, a public drawing room, a ladies' drawing room, ladies' and gentlemen's reading and correspondence rooms, billiard, bagatelle and smoke rooms, a recreation and concert hall, a Turkish bath, a large sea-water plunge bath, and ladies' and gentlemen's treatment areas. There were to be high but heated corridors, the vestibule and entrance hall were to be of 'noble dimensions', and the place was to be well lit and decorated with modern stained glass. Verandas, a winter garden and fernery, and hydraulic lifts were also selling points. And, of course, there was the site itself, described by the *Oban Times* on 28 May 1881 as 'perhaps the best that could possibly be obtained in the Kingdom': a stunning site high above Oban Bay with just a slightly different prospect over Kerrera, Mull and Lismore to the one which would be enjoyed in a few years' time by that other magnificent edifice, McCaig's tower.

All of this magnificence was to come within the budget – but the budget put forward by the architect had not yet been realised. There was a plan to borrow on the security of the buildings, taking out a mortgage from investors, and even at this stage, fears were expressed about the possibility of escalating costs. Mr Hunter of Denny, who asked sensible questions along these lines, was assured that Ford-Mackenzie's plans had been measured 'with the utmost care and precision'. There were further assurances that the tendering was done on a better system than the one operated in Glasgow, with the implication that there would be no 'hidden costs'.

And so the tenders were considered and Robert McAlpine and Company of Hamilton, as the company was then known, were contracted to carry out excavation of the site, and the brickwork, masonry and plaster work; J. MacCormack and Company of Glasgow were hired for the carpentry and joinery work. Both companies agreed to take large amounts of their contract price in Oban Hills shares. Smaller shares were also given to William Anderson, the Glasgow plumber contracted to work on the project; D. G. Brown, a Glasgow painter; and Alexander Dobson, the Edinburgh slater who would be the last man on site. Only the glazier did not receive shares as part payment of his contract.

In June 1881 the boundary lines were mapped off and flagged. Palm trees were uprooted and the site was cleared for action. By the end of the month, problems were already being encountered, but while the contractors struggled to blast through difficult rock on the face of the hill, the *Glasgow Evening Times* was doing a magnificent public relations exercise in describing the 'marvellous views' from the site, and this was followed up in August in the *North British Daily Mail* by an article which exclaimed that the hydropathic 'promises to be one of the great features of the town of Oban'. By now, McAlpines had blasted a carriageway to the site, laid concrete foundations, installed a steam engine to the top of the hill, and laid a line of rails to the lower part of the town so that building materials could be winched up on wagons loaded at the still spanking-new goods station. This tramline was 230 yards long and cost £140 to make, but it was estimated that the savings on cartage would make this an economical alternative.

By 7 September, the walls were completed up to the first storey, according to the *Evening Times* of that day, and 180 men were employed. It was estimated that the workforce would rise to 300 as soon as the men could be found, so that all the daylight hours could be used before winter set in. In late October, the second storey had been reached, and by December the newly-reached third floor created quite a spectacle from the water. A gale on 21 November had caused no damage, but on 7 January 1882, the *Oban Times* reported a hurricane described as 'the storm of this generation'. New tenements of shops and houses at Breadalbane Place had been blown down, but only a 'small portion' of the front of the hydropathic had been carried away. Towards the end of February a more serious incident for the contractors occurred: two men, George Scott from Selkirk and John Chisholm from Galashiels, fell 30

feet from scaffolding when a portion of the wall at the north-east corner
of the hydropathic fell. A third man escaped injury, but two doctors,
Campbell and McKelvie, had to be called to the site. These same doctors were called again in April when another mason, John McLachlan
from Dundee, was knocked off a portion of the wall he was building
by a crane. By June, when the Oban Hills Company had expected to
be preparing to open, the *North British Daily Mail* commented, 'there
appears to be a hitch somewhere, as no workmen have been seen near it
for some days past'. A week later, the same publication was saying that
work on the hydropathic was at a standstill, 'a fact that must rejoice the
hearts of hotel keepers in the town, to whom it must ultimately prove a
formidable rival'. However, by the end of June work had resumed, with
the roof beginning to be put in place and the grounds being developed.
The drains, however, were causing problems and the by now carping
Daily Mail saw it as 'a huge ruins [sic] without a ruin's generally picturesque effect'. Rumours spread throughout the summer of 1882 that an
English company had taken over the project, and in September it was
described as 'a building of gigantic proportions which remains in an
unfinished state'.

Oban hydropathic, 'a monument to the folly of commencing to
build without counting the cost'. A month before McCaig went
to the General Assembly, the investors were licking their wounds.
Michael Hopkin Collection.

In December the contractors moved out. The movable plant was gone, the window openings were boarded up, the slater came and carried away all the slates on the ground, and, although there was sarking on the roof timbers, much of the building remained unslated. Feisty young Duncan Cameron, editor of the *Oban Times*, said on 2 December 1882, 'The whole building is a monument to the folly of commencing to build without counting the cost.' On 20 December, Oban Hills Hydropathic Sanatorium Co. Ltd. was 'wound up voluntarily'.

By April 1883, a month before the Reverend Donald McCaig was planning his first ever visit to the General Assembly of the Church of Scotland in almost three decades as a minister, the private citizens who had invested their money were counting the cost of the hydropathic. In the fullness of time, William Gillies, the distiller who owned the site until he feued it to the company in April 1882, was bankrupted, according to the Argyll Sasines.

At the same time as the Presbytery of Lorn was holding its meetings to compose a proposal for a Celtic Church in the Highlands, the *Oban Times* was condemning the outcome of the hydropathic disaster, pointing out that it had irretrievably ruined the landscape, illustrating 'how hideously and completely natural beauties can be deformed'. Was a plan already in Donald McCaig's mind to raise the issue of bringing St Andrews to this site? He would tell the General Assembly that Scotland was lopsided in the distribution of its universities: three in the east, one (Glasgow) in the west, none north of the Highland line. St Andrews was situated in some venerable but at that time primitive and insanitary buildings. Here was a new building of generous – indeed, determinedly luxurious – proportions ideally suited to his idea.

No one took him up on it. He may have been described as the star of the show in Edinburgh, but some very evidently saw him as the comic turn – a man with no substance. The Highlands were not a popular cause, as the election result two years later would confirm. As a journalist on the city-centric *Evening Express* pointed out, 'The fact is, Ireland has a big land question on, and the Highlands of Scotland persist in having their turn. So with universities. Oban is not going to be any further behind than it can help. Mr McCaig would transfer St Andrew's to Oban and he thinks the result would be for the health alike of the Principal and of the University.' Generously, he suggested that instead of moving the mountain to Mohammed, a fifth university should be opened,

Neither hydropathic hotel not Highland university, today the ruin
still looms over Oban.

with McCaig as principal. 'That', he wrote, with much less irony than
in his opening paragraphs, 'would refresh the Highlands for a long time
to come, and furnish a complete antidote to the Catholic institution at
Fort Augustus [about which McCaig had been very complimentary in
his address to the Assembly]'.

In fact, Donald McCaig was in no fit state to be principal of a university, an MP, or, indeed, a minister. His health was failing even while he
wrestled with his decision to stand for Westminster. In 1884 he and his
Oban-councillor brother Dugald fought on behalf of the common man
against the might of the railway company, which had fenced off access
to Drumvargie Well, on Glenshellach Road. The case went to the Court
of Session but proceedings were later dropped. After the 1885 election,
Donald went back to Muckairn. He had continued to put out editions
of his Gaelic magazine the *Highland Claymore* from 1879 to 1882, and
he now produced a book of poems, *The Last Enemy*. But there came a
final illness, in which he was looked after by one of the sisters. He died
at 5 o'clock on the morning of 11 April 1886 at the age of just fifty-nine.

His last words were, 'I shall soon know all the mysteries.' At his funeral in Pennyfuir cemetery, J. S. and Major McCaig took two of the cords, and among the others paying homage were Oban's Provost Menzies, Campbell of Lochnell and Campbell of Dunstaffnage.

They may have laughed at his curious ideas in Edinburgh, but Donald McCaig was a man of principle whose life's work – like that of the author of Oban's more obvious curiosity – was for the common good.

6

SLATED

Dwelly's Gaelic to English Dictionary gives two meanings for the word *uaigh*; neither sounds welcoming. The first choice is a tomb, grave or sepulchre. The second is den, cave or cavern. In his report on the parish of Jura and Colonsay for the *First Statistical Account of Scotland* in 1799, the Rev. Francis Stewart refers to 'Balnahuaigh', which could translate as 'the place of the tomb'. Today, this tiny island is known as Belnahua – uninhabited since World War I and a curious example of how relentless nature can be when left to her own devices. With no domestic animals to graze the grass and scant human footsteps treading its mile-round circumference, the machair has become a thick, tangled mattress through which no princess could claim to sense a pea.

Yet peas there are – metaphorically speaking. Beneath this soft, luxurious quilt lies the imprint of two centuries of hard labour, the trace of austere lives ruled by the elements and the employers, each equally demanding. The shells of the houses remain. The names of once-respected engineering companies stamped on the rusting machinery have outlived the names of those who worked here, went to school here, washed laundry in water brought from neighbouring Luing, and cooked meagre meals of herring and tatties. This was a slate island, and, according to historian Nigel Tranter, it had its back broken by the quarrymen. Standing on the metre-thick machair in the 'main street' of the island, it seems more likely that the quarrymen, and their wives and children, had their spirit broken by Belnahua.

There is a poem by Rachel Field which begins 'If once you have slept on an island, you'll never be quite the same.' The change which some islands offer is serenity gifted through peace and tranquillity. Belnahua, buffeted by the sea and the winds, overshadowed from the south by the lowering cliffs of Scarba, and dominated by the threatening deep maws of the slate quarries at its heart, could surely have engendered little more than tension, agitation, fear and anxiety. There is no joy to be seen on

Boys at the landing jetty on the south shore of Belnahua in the 1890s. *Mackenzie Collection, Scottish Slate Islands Heritage Trust.*

the faces of two boys caught on camera in the 1890s as they sit on the seaweed-covered rocks watching the boats come into the tricky landing place. Childhood was not invented for the youngsters of Belnahua.

Mud is not always seen as an attractive commodity, but under certain circumstances it can be transformed into something of great usefulness, such as slate. Some 440 million years ago, during the Ordovician period, the mud on the bottom of a shallow sea south of what today is Oban was hugely disturbed by the cataclysmic eruptions which created the world as we know it. Layers of it became compressed and heated, and were transformed into slate and schists. These were further agitated around 55 million years ago by volcanic eruptions on the island of Mull which pushed molten lava between the slate beds.

No one knows when man discovered that slate was a commodity from which floors and roofs could be made, and upon which he could write, or chop food. Perhaps many who passed by the islands south of Oban during the past six or seven thousand years used slate in small amounts for their own purposes. If nothing else, they would have been attracted by the sparkling iron pyrites – fool's gold – which are embedded in the blue-black slate. Slabs of slate were certainly used in medieval times as gravestones. Then it became a commercial commodity, enriching the fortunes of local landlords. For at least four centuries, slate was quarried on the islands of Easdale, Luing, Seil and Belnahua. Dean Munro mentions such quarrying in the middle of the 1500s, and there is a date in the *Old Statistical Account* for Jura of 1632 as the start of commercial quarrying on Belnahua. The Easdale slate belt was eventually producing eight million slates a year, which were being exported all around the world and used to roof prestigious buildings in Scotland, including Glasgow Cathedral.

Most of the area was owned by the Breadalbane family, but Belnahua somehow escaped this dragnet. When John Campbell, Earl of Breadalbane, and three Campbell partners set up the Marble and Slate Quarrying Company of Netherlorn in 1745, Belnahua, in the parish of Jura, was not part of the operation. There were, however, twenty-eight families living on the island, according to the 1791–99 *Statistical Account of Scotland*, Vol. 20, 'The Western Isles', and about half of the thirty men were employed quarrying slate, for which they were 'paid by the piece, or at so much the thousand slate'. When Breadalbane and his kinsmen set up the Netherlorn company, the Stevenson brothers were

Fool's gold – cubes of iron pyrites with facets up to 4 x 4 mm
– may have attracted people to the island from the earliest times.

building their own commercial empire in Oban, and by the early years of the nineteenth century Thomas Stevenson, a distiller and descendant of the entrepreneurial brothers, was shipping slate from quarries at Belnahua and Phladda – today known as little more than the lighthouse island of Fladda – to Campbeltown.

This Stevenson was not, however, as successful in his dealings as his forebears had been. He had some curious ideas: he had travelled to South America, held heritable property in Buenos Aires, and was, for a while, one of a select band of people trying to breed alpaca in Britain for the manufacture of worsted. The first alpaca were brought to Britain in 1809 by Mr de Tastelet of Essex. The Duchess of York had several as pets, but, in 1817 a gentleman named Burnett managed to rear fifteen young ones in Berkshire, and in 1825 Viscount Ingentre not only succeeded in getting his alpaca to breed but managed to shear their fine coats twice. Mr Stevenson created what was known as a llama park in Oban, but his alpaca – for that is what his animals were – did not flourish, according to the 1844 *New Statistical Account*. Nor did his slate business on Belnahua. At successive Courts of Session, in 1829, 1830 and 1831, he went through bankruptcy procedures and the Belnahua property was under scrutiny. Utensils were valued, including machinery for draining quarries. The court recommended that the quarrymen's employment should continue and set up a credit and debit system to ensure their payment.

At this time there were around 140 people living on Belnahua. The census figure for 1861 was 142 – by 1881 it would rise to to 153 – a lot of people living in just 23 little terraced houses sandwiched between a treacherous sea and even more treacherous quarries which had to be pumped night and day to keep them from flooding. In the 1860s the Shaw family were tacksmen, or factors, of the slate quarries. There were two brothers sharing the job: John and Hugh, who lived in the imaginatively named House 1 and House 2. John Shaw had six children at the time of the 1861 census and Hugh had two little daughters and a baby son, and the Shaw's mother lived with him – a widow in her late seventies. Each family had a servant: young girls in their early teens whose main work may well have been to keep the children from drowning in the sea or falling into a quarry.

The Shaws had a history in slate. James Shaw, John and Hugh's grandfather, had moved from Bunessan on Mull to Netherlorn in the 1720s to work on the land, and one of his sons, Angus, who was born around

Around 140 people were shoehorned into these tiny cottages on
Belnahua in 1861.

the time that the Netherlorn slate company was being set up, grew up to
be a pilot guiding sailing barques into Easdale harbour to collect slate.
Two of his sons, John and Hugh, were raised in the slate industry, according to John's grandson Angus, a well-known Scottish journalist and
raconteur of the mid twentieth century. John was born in 1814 and
travelled around working in the Scottish slate industry. By the 1860s,
he and his brother Hugh had moved to Belnahua, and they brought up
their families to work with the slate too. John eventually crossed the mile
of water to neighbouring Luing, where he managed the slate quarries
at Cullipool, owned by a Glasgow company calling itself the Cullipool
Slate Quarries Company.

The brothers eventually bought and operated the Belnahua quarries
until the outbreak of the Great War, when the island was sold to a family
called Gillies, and subsequently to Paul Carling. But Mr Gillies bought
a deserted island: the men had gone off to war and there was no reason
for the women and children to stay. Indeed, there was no possibility: the
water had to be brought from a burn on Luing, and the post came once a
week from Cullipool on the same neighbouring island after 1898. There
may have been a tethered cow on Belnahua, but roaming animals would
have been a danger to themselves. One map does identify an area in the

northern part of the island as cultivated, but if kale or potatoes were ever grown there, they would have come out of the ground ready salted. It certainly doesn't seem as if there would have been room enough for the slate, the pumping machinery, the houses, the school room *and* plots big enough to grow vegetables for the whole population, supposing any crop would have flourished in those harsh conditions. Provisions were shipped from elsewhere, to be sold in the tiny shop.

One of the many curious aspects of today's Belnahua is that there is no sign of past domesticity – only a few yogurt pots left by inconsiderate modern yachtsmen. There are no fragments of the lives lived out here. No rusting pans, no broken crockery, no rotting chairs. The archaeologists of the future may find the final remains of the houses, the

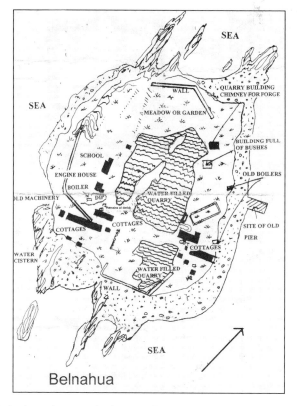

Belnahua, showing the layout of the cottages, the quarries and landing areas, and the area assumed to have been meadow or garden. *Scottish Slate Islands Heritage Trust.*

machinery, and even the already much disintegrated jetty, but none of the domestic detritus which has given us clues throughout Argyll to the lifestyles, cultures and beliefs of Iron Age families, Viking raiders and farmers, and medieval aristocracy. Angus Shaw, whose childhood was lived out on Luing, looked across at Belnahua with affection, and the Shaws may have lived there in comparative ease. However, it is all too easy to conclude that there was so little material comfort in the other, stark, box-like homes of that island that when the women were evacuated to live on Luing and elsewhere they were able to carry every last thread and shard with them in the boats. It also is easy to believe that they left with more relief than sorrow. They would miss their men and fear for them as they fought on Flanders Field, but possibly this new fear was no greater than that which they had felt subconsciously every day their fathers, brothers, husbands and sons went to quarry the slate.

In the Easdale Museum, which charts the history of the main slate islands, there are images of men without any safety equipment – had any been invented then? – perched high on quarry walls or dangling on the ends of ropes. Perhaps the Shaws, who had themselves experienced these dangers at first hand, offered better working practices on the little island of Belnahua than those instituted on Easdale, Luing and elsewhere in the Breadalbane slate empire. In 1887 there were mass meetings of that empire's quarrymen after a serious accident. Men were crushed in a fatal accident; families complained that they were in 'a starving condition'; a letter to the *Oban Times* pointed out the irony of the Marquess of Breadalbane being president of the Scottish Liberal Association, asking, 'How can there be such serfdom and slavery under him?' A further irony came in the flurry of letters to the editor complaining about a new luxury hotel at Easdale which might 'lure' these underpaid men into sampling its pleasures. As unlikely as it might have been that any Easdale worker would have ventured into such well-appointed 'first class Highland accommodation' or been able to pay for anything on the premises, they and their families were at least nearer 'civilisation'. Indeed, by the turn of the century omnibuses ran from Easdale to Oban and a telephone had been installed in the area which could summon medical help in case of accidents in the quarries. On Belnahua, right up until the day the women were evacuated in the First World War, life remained as isolated and as primitive as it must have been when the intrepid Pennant visited the Slate Islands in 1772.

Belnahua was not even mentioned by Pennant, nor, indeed, by Martin Martin on his tour of the islands seventy years previously which informed his book *Curiosities of Art and Nature*. Low and unlovely, it was not high on anyone's agenda. Even the Church casually pushed it, in an administrative sense, from pillar to post, transferring the island from the parish of Jura to the parish of Kilbrandon and Kilchattan in the middle of the nineteenth century. The 1861 census gives a sense of the make-up of the community. Peter McLachlan, who lived at House 3, Belnahua, with his wife Matilda, was a fisherman. He was sixty-six and Matilda was sixty, and perhaps he remained on Belnahua to provide fish for the islanders. There would certainly have been no prospect of retirement. Niel McLachlan at House 5 was most likely a relative. This eighty-year-old was registered in the 1861 census as a pauper, and he lived with his wife

Some fished, some looked after the machinery and some were paupers, but most of those landing on Belnahua the 1890s worked the island's quarries. *Mackenzie Collection, Scottish Slate Islands Heritage Trust.*

Catherine and their teenage granddaughter, who most probably looked after the elderly couple. Still more McLachlans lived at House 16, and Peter and two of his teenage sons, Arthur and John, were all quarriers. A daughter and two more sons were at school, and there were two little ones: Isabella and Niel, aged four and two. No wife is named. Christine Livingston at House 12 was a quarryman's widow. Christine had three quarrier sons and a daughter to look after her, but some women on their own were less fortunate. At House 7 lived Ann Brown, unmarried and a former country servant, and Mary James, also unmarried and also a former servant, who in 1861 were both paupers. Also living in the house was Allan Brown, a 32-year-old smith, his wife Mary and their three young children. Ann must have been an aunt, and these extended family relationships helped everyone to survive.

Families were large, but in 1861 they were well enough educated. There was a school on the island and Malcolm McDougall, a lodger with the large McLugash family at House 6, was the teacher. Isabella looked after her husband, Archibald, and three quarrier sons as well as Mr McDougall and three younger children. Sharing the house was Alexander May, a labourer, and his eleven-year-old niece Catherine, who was described as a domestic servant. Poor Catherine did the housework while the daughter of the family, twelve-year-old Susan McLugash, went across to the school. Many of the grown-up women were described as domestic servants: at House 11 Archibald MacDonald was head of a household shared with his older and younger brothers, while their sister was described as a servant. Archie attended the engine in the quarry, older brother Donald was a boat-builder and younger brother Niel was engine-keeper. There were fishermen in the McPhail family at House 16, and the Flemings at House 19 included two seamen and a fisherman. Mrs McPhail at House 22 was a fisherman's widow.

One wonders if those who were not quarrymen chose to live there, or were they perhaps too poor to move elsewhere? Regardless, it was the quarries which dominated the life of the island, and only the quarries have a presence on the island today. The people who passed their lives here to the constant clanking of the pumps which kept the sea from the two cavernous slate pits are now nothing more than census lists in libraries.

Their departure left the way clear for the voles, the otters and the ever-thickening carpet of grasses and flowers which is slowly swallowing

Hairy bindweed now grows in profusion on the ungrazed and
uninhabited island of Belnahua.

up the past. The taxonomist Dr Crinan Alexander of the Royal Botanic
Garden in Edinburgh accompanied this author to Belnahua. These were
his impressions:

> The vegetation on Belnahua conveys the strong, Marie Celeste-like im-
> pression that the hand of man was formerly much more in control.
> Desolate ruined buildings are choked with brambles and the surround-
> ing areas of shattered slate are infested with nettles, creeping buttercup
> and waving cocksfoot grass. The ancient dinosaur-like remains of the
> slate-processing machinery have been similarly invaded and are also em-
> braced by corky elder branches festooned with slightly sinister Judas' ear
> fungus. In what might once have been a paddock just north of one of
> the houses, the lush fescue grasses, long ungrazed, have been combed by
> the wind into a deep springy mattress over which it is hard to proceed
> without collapsing, the more so as piles of slate and other snares lie
> concealed underneath.
>
> Bounding this area to the east is a low overgrown wall on which flour-
> ishes hairy bindweed; its impressive pale pink trumpets spilling down
> onto the deep grass and catching the eye from some way off. Though
> widely naturalised it is thought to be 'of garden origin' in Britain, so did

the slate quarriers grow it in their gardens or has it arrived since their time with curious visitors or perhaps on birds' feet?

On the very exposed fin-like ridge near the SW corner of the island conditions are more acidic as betrayed by a dense covering of heathers, especially on the slightly more sheltered eastern slope, which allows access to the summit. Frustratingly out of reach, dangling among honeysuckle and ivy above the shallow cave at the south end of this ridge is a rose with bright red hips. The wind was so strong during our visit that no adequate view was to be had, even through binoculars. It might have been one of the downy roses, a dog rose or perhaps an escaped Japanese rose with densely prickly stems, which is often found in gardens in these parts. The burnet or Scots rose with its characteristic black hips is also recorded in this area though we saw no evidence of it. Just west of the ridge is a low lying valley with many shallow pools, home to Brookweed (*Samolus valerandi*), occasionally found in such areas close to the sea, though more often overlooked.

Shelter is hard to find and this no doubt accounts for the lack of any trees other than elder, which some regard as never more than a well-grown shrub anyway. Even birch, that enthusiastic coloniser of ungrazed areas, seems not to have gained a foothold. The cliffy margins of the extensive flooded quarries which occupy much of the centre of the island provide

View from a quarrier's window: the fin-like ridge of the island, machinery to pump water out of the quarries, the boiler house and, in the distance, the school.

The name on this abandoned pump machinery has outlasted the
names of the families who lived on Belnahua, 'place of the tomb'.

shelter for marsh ragwort and other moisture-loving plants and there is a
little more shelter in the form of an extensive arc of wall at the north end
of the island, presumably designed to prevent the quarries from inunda-
tion by the sea. This man-made dyke finds its natural counterpart in a
dolerite dyke emerging from the sea near the north-west corner, one of
hundreds which radiated out from the volcanoes of Mull in the Tertiary
period, about 3.5 million years ago.

The phrase 'shelter is hard to find' paints the most vivid picture of this
island today, and in the era when women and children huddled in the
flimsy houses on the shore of Belnahua while their menfolk struggled
to quarry the slate in the face of savage elements. It was part of a group
of islands which, as they say, 'roofed the world', while the human rights
due to their inhabitants were ignored. Man's curious will to survive was
their only protection in this 'place of the tomb'.

7

COLUMBA AND A LOST CACHE

When the Rev. Donald McCaig floated his idea of a university in Oban, the newspaper commentators had a field day. Irony dripped from their pens as they sought one hundred and one ways to belittle the concept of the Highlands having any need for such an academic establishment. Rough rude Highlanders were not educated, did not even understand the English language, and had no use for Virgil, Homer, Livy or Pliny. The *Oban Times* had to remind the world that Mr McCaig had himself attended three of Scotland's universities and had gained high honours at them all. This was not to mention the hundreds of scholars from throughout the Highlands and Islands who over the centuries had studied not only at Scotland's four universities but at some of Europe's most prestigious academic centres before going on to enrich the world in many spheres with their intellect.

Nor was this pursuit of learning a modern phenomenon dating from the period of the Enlightenment, when Scotland's scholars and philosophers contributed equally alongside those of France to the blossoming of knowledge. It is said that the Druids established a centre of learning on Innis nam Druidneach, renamed Iona by Columba and his followers when they set up their monastic nerve centre there. This centre of learning became a 'university' which between the sixth and eighth centuries rivalled any in Europe. Its library contained not only the most beautiful of books, but the most learnèd – and the most rare. It is only natural to imagine that such a library would only contain works transcribed and lavishly illustrated by the monks, but the Iona library is also believed to have contained some of the world's most precious books, including those of the great Greek and Roman philosophers and scholars. The curious legend which clings to that library is that its contents were saved and hidden on Cairnburgh Mor in the Treshnish Isles. Perhaps most curious of all is the idea that the lost books of Livy's *History of Rome* were among the books cached on Cairnburgh. It is just as possible that

The lost manuscripts of Pliny are said to be among those taken
from Iona to Cairnburgh Mor.

lost manuscripts of Pliny the Elder were also part of that great library,
and that while some of his manuscripts were taken east to Northumbria
– some ended up in the possession of the Venerable Bede – others were
taken for safe keeping to Cairnburgh Mor – and, like the lost books of
Livy's *History of Rome*, never seen again.

That wonderful chronicler of the traditions of the Western Isles, Otta
F. Swire, says in her book *The Inner Hebrides and Their Legends* that it
was during the raids of the Norse pirates – who raided Iona four times
between 795 and 825 – that the library was removed and that 'many of
the precious books, wrapped in hides, were buried on the small rocky
islet of Cairn a'burgh'. According to the Hebridean Trust, which today
manages the Treshnish Isles, Cairnburgh Mor was probably occupied
from Viking times, but the trust's version of the fable is that 'the treasures
of Iona were buried there to avoid depredation during the Reformation
and that they may still be lost somewhere on the islands'.

This version of the legend was favoured by Peter MacNab, a Mull man who wrote about the islands of Mull and Iona throughout his lifetime. It was his contention that those books which survived the Viking raids and had not been removed to Ireland for safety were kept on the island until the Reformation when, under an Act of 1561, Iona was seen as a stronghold of the Church of Rome and attacked as such. The Synod of Argyll sent out orders for the island to be cleared of all 'papish' relics. Just as in other parts of Argyll, on the sacred isle of Iona crosses were smashed or thrown into the sea, graves were desecrated and the library was burned and destroyed. Monks who fled the island took some of the treasures with them. Books and reliquaries were found places of safe keeping not only in Scotland and Ireland but in Paris and Rome. MacNab believed that some items were hidden on Cairnburgh Mor, but that in the seventeenth century, when bloody civil war waged for decades, either Cromwell's troops or the Covenanters discovered the cache and destroyed it.

It is hardly surprising that, as with most traditions, there are discrepancies: did the famous library disappear in the ninth or the seventeenth century? Did it come under attack from Norse raiders or Presbyterian zealots? Were its remnants destroyed by Puritans or Covenanters? Or did they in fact survive?

What is perhaps still more curious than whether precious books were hidden somewhere on a relatively inaccessible fortified rock in the Treshnish is how the books got to Iona in the first instance. The exquisite illustrated books which are today known as the *Book of Kells*, and held at Trinity College, Dublin, were created on Iona by the monks. The older manuscripts, however, were said to have come from Rome when the empire had a knife at its throat and the city was finally sacked and destroyed.

The Rev. Donald Campbell, minister of Kilfinichen and Kilviceuen in the Presbytery of Mull, wrote in his extensive footnotes to the 1834–45 *Statistical Accounts of Scotland* that the Druids' library had been substantially added to by Fergus II, a descendant of Erc the Antrim prince who had parcelled out Argyll between his three sons. Fergus II, according to the early historian Boethius, fought alongside Alaric the Goth at the sack of Rome in 410. There must have been unimaginable treasures to loot, but Fergus chose to take a chest of Greek, Roman and Persian books back to the library on Innis nam Druidneach, presenting it to the theological college there. In one of many ironic twists in the tale, Columba went

St Columba left Ireland because of a battle over a book. His monastery on Iona incorporated an extensive library founded by the
Druids. Icon by Aidan Hart.

to Scotland more than a century later – he established his monastery
in Iona in 563 – because of a disputed book, and found a library well
stocked with books by the most respected authors in the world.

Columba, the 'Dove of the Church' as he was known and the great-
great-grandson of the Irish king Niall of the Nine Hostages, had left
his own country as a penance after seeing men die in a battle over the
copyright of a psalter. St Finnian claimed Columba had tried to pass the
psalter off as his own work, and, after a fierce battle fought over the issue
in 561, Columba went to Scotland vowing to convert as many as had
been killed in the conflict. As a focus for his mission, he was granted the
island of Iona by Conal, 5th King of the Dalriadan Scots and a distant
relation. During his time there, according to his biographer Adomnan,
the ninth-century abbot of Iona, Columba personally transcribed more
than three hundred books as well as writing some of his own. If a fine
library containing classical masterpieces already existed when he arrived
there, it is no wonder that Columba was so quickly able to establish a
centre of learning. It was Irish monks from Iona who then founded a
similar scholarly centre in Northumbria, and the Venerable Bede was

educated in that tradition at Wearmouth monastery and then at Jarrow. According to M. L. W. Laistner, MA, Fellow of the Royal History Society, in a 1933 paper, Bede certainly used the second book of Pliny the Elder's *Natural History* and knew other parts of the work. Whatever happened to the works of Livy aside, could it have been that some volumes of Pliny were taken by the monks from Iona to Northumbria?

And if Fergus II had indeed gifted looted books to the Druids, what exactly did they get? Titus Livius, as the Romans knew Livy, was born near Padua some sixty years before the birth of Christ, and, having lived much of his life in Rome, he returned north and died in his home city in AD 17. Despite his reputation as an author, Livy's only work to have survived was his *History of Rome* ('Ab Urbe Condita'), which covered the period from the city's foundation to 9 BC. He wrote 142 'books' or scrolls, but only 35 survived, along with short summaries of most of the rest of his works. A fragment of the ninety-first book was discovered in the Vatican library in 1772. Other previously unknown material was discovered in Egypt in 1900. That some of the lost books of Livy had found their way to Iona was, however, sufficiently accepted that in the fifteenth-century Aeneas Sylvius, who was to become Pope Pius II, intended to visit the Iona library during a visit to Scotland.

Enea Silvio Piccolomini – one of a number of Piccolomini to become Popes – known by his Latin name of Aeneas Sylvius, was born on 18 October 1405. He was a bright scholar who excelled in literature, poetry, oratory, history and law. After living the typical life of a student, he reformed enough to be taken on as secretary to Cardinal Nicholas Albergati and as such travelled throughout Europe. The cardinal was Eugene IV's legate in Scotland, and, in 1435, he sent Piccolomini on a secret mission to that cold northern country. In an attempt to end the One Hundred Years' War between England and France, Albergati instructed Piccolomini to try to persuade King James I of Scotland to launch an attack on England. Piccolomini also wanted to meet with a Scottish archdeacon in London, William Croyser, who had been condemned for treason and denied his office in the papal councils of Florence. It was a difficult journey for this brilliant young negotiator. He was arrested in Calais, and when he went to London on his release, was not allowed to travel overland from there to the Scottish border. As he tried to sail to Scotland, storms blew him off course towards Norway. Even as he neared his destination, there were violent squalls in the Firth of Forth. His boat

Enea Silvio Piccolomini, who became Pope Pius II, wanted to
visit the Iona library in 1435 but was distracted during his visit to
Scotland. *Getty Images.*

eventually pitched up near Dunbar, from whence he walked barefoot in
the snow to the Shrine of Our Lady at Whitekirk, Haddington, to give
thanks for having survived the perilous journey.

Piccolomini's letters and diaries show that he was more than seven
months in Scotland. His official mission was a failure, and Mr Campbell says in his footnotes to the Kilfinichen and Kilviceuen *Statistical
Account* that he was also unable to visit the Iona library in search of the
lost books of Livy because of the death of James I, who had been assas-
sinated at Friars Preachers Monastery in Perth on 21 February 1437,
having failed to escape from his attackers, running instead into a sewer
which was blocked by tennis balls. However, the dates do not fit, so
this perhaps was not the real reason for Piccolomini not having made
what would have been an arduous journey to Iona. However, during
his stay in a country which he described as economically and culturally
depressed, he did find time, according to his personal papers, to father
a child by a Scottish woman. In 1458 he was elected pope, and, unlike
modern popes he would not have the chance to travel again to Scotland
to investigate the Iona library. Instead, his nephew, who followed him as
Pius III, created the Piccolomini Library in the Sienna duomo to commemorate his uncle's work as a peacemaker.

The idea that the library at Iona was lost during the four intense
Norwegian raids on the island between 795 and 825 must lose much

credibility in view of this continued interest in it some 600 years later. King Malcolm and the saintly Margaret had rebuilt Iona monastery during their reign, and the books and manuscripts which survived were interesting enough to engage the attention of a future pope. A century after Piccolomini had been too preoccupied to visit Iona, a small parcel of books was taken to Aberdeen to be examined by scholars there. The Rev. Donald Campbell wrote in his parish statistical account that this 1525 exposition of some of the ancient Iona manuscripts led the intellectuals at the university to say the fragile fragments were more in the style of Sallust, a supporter of Julius Caesar who wrote histories of his career during his retirement between 78 and 67 BC, than Livy. Within decades, the new Protestant Church had been established in Scotland. If the theory that the library was destroyed in the fury which followed the Reformation is true, then this attempt in those troubled pre-Reformation years to identify and perhaps preserve its contents by engaging the scholars in Aberdeen symbolises not only the death throes of the library, but also a snapping of the intellectual thread that stretched back to the greatest intellects which the ancients had to offer.

All traditional sources suggest that the Iona collection most certainly included Livy's lost books and possibly the works of Pliny the Elder, the best-selling author of his time. Larcius Licinus, the praetorium legate of Hispana Tarraconensis, bid £3,200 for 160 volumes of Pliny, which converted into the currency values of today far outstrips the million-pound advances paid to top 21st-century novelists. The only work which survives today is his *Natural History* series, and even that is not complete. Where did his manuscripts go? There are records of some: in the middle of the third century, an abstract of some geographical work was produced by Solinus; in the early fourth century, some medical passages were collected in *Medicia Plinii*; and early in the eighth century, the English Christian leader the Venerable Bede was in possession of what was described as a manuscript of the whole of *Natural History*. Some manuscripts were in France in the hands of Charlemagne in the ninth century and later in a monastery at Bescançon, and these fragments are now held in Rome, Paris and Leiden. But books were certainly lost, and it is surely not over-imaginative to surmise that at some time they sat alongside Livy's lost books on the island of Iona.

In the eighteenth century, the traveller Thomas Pennant, convinced that the library 'must have been invaluable', offered another theory concerning the whereabouts of its contents. Rather than branding the Vikings as barbarians who might have destroyed the books, he suggested that during the time that the Norwegians ruled the Western Isles of Scotland they may have taken the books home for safe-keeping. Pennant, who travelled in the Western Isles in the 1770s, thought that 'numbers of the records of the Hebrides were preserved at Drontheim, till they were destroyed by the great fire which happened in that city'.

The most compelling theory, however, is that they were hidden on Cairnburgh Mor, wrapped in hide or otherwise, and that the monks hid the books there in the sixteenth rather than the ninth century. The castle on Cairnburgh Mor and Cairnburgh Beg, with ancilliary buildings on Cairnburgh Beg, was not on record as a fortification until the thirteenth century, when it was briefly regarded as royal by both the Norwegian and Scottish crowns. In 1654, the atlas-maker Blaeu referred to 'the two [islands] called Cairn na Burgh, larger and smaller, walled in by sheer cliffs and the cruelly rushing waters of a very violent tide, so that by the natural defence and fortification both are safe from every enemy and attack and stand impregnable'. The Royal Commission on the Ancient and Historical Monuments of Scotland describes the natural fortification of the twin islands as 'formidable' and the twin castle spread across the two Treshnish islands as 'remarkable'. This is the sort of place where the desperate would hide the priceless.

Blaeu the map-maker referred to Cairnburgh Mor and Beg as 'safe from every enemy and attack'. A good hiding place for precious treasure. *Crown Copyright © Royal Commission on the Ancient and Historical Monuments of Scotland.*

There is no safe anchorage even in summer, and the two islands – Mor and Beg (big and small) – are separated by a channel where strong tides mean treacherous landings. Within this dangerous channel, access to the islands can only be made by a small boat. Basalt cliffs rise over 100 feet above sea level, and at the top, on the gentle green slope of about 5 acres, sits a castle and chapel made from rubble masonry with dressings of stones quarried at Carsaig on Mull. Barracks on this grassy knoll housed very lonely and probably very frightened soldiers over a period of five centuries as power surged back and forth between countries, clans and religious factions. The castle of 'Kiarnaborg' was first mentioned in 1249 when King Haakon of Norway put Ewen, Lord of Lorn, in charge of it and three other fortifications. It became a Scottish royal castle after the Treaty of Perth in 1266 and went into the hands of Angus Og of Islay in the following century. MacDougalls ceded the castle to John of Islay in 1354 on condition that he would not allow MacKinnons to hold it. By the fifteenth century, it was the MacLeans of Duart who possessed the fortifications on the two islands in the Treshnish, but they rebelled against the king and in 1504 Cairnburgh Mor and Beg were besieged by a royal expeditionary force from the naval base at Dumbarton. Lachlan MacLean regained the islands in 1513 and was later officially reinstated.

View from 'impregnable' Cairnburgh Castle. *Crown Copyright © Royal Commission on the Ancient and Historical Monuments of Scotland.*

A new archaeological dig is planned on Cairnburgh Mor. Iona Abbey has been restored: the books may yet be returned. Pen and ink sketch by R. Willow, 1834.

MacLeans held the islands in the cruel months when the iconoclastic Protestants angrily smashed their way across Iona.

During the British Civil Wars, the MacLeans had Royalist sympathies and the castle again came under siege. General David Leslie, Lord Newark, a professional soldier who had fought for the Swedes in the Thirty Years' War, captured the castle in 1647. He had returned to Scotland at the start of the Civil Wars to command the armies of the Scottish Covenanter government. He was responsible for routing the main Royalist forces under the Duke of Montrose in 1645, and in 1647 he roamed the western seaboard from the Treshnish to Dunaverty at the tip of Kintyre, wreaking vengeance as he went. He left Cairnburgh in the hands of Hector MacLean of Torloisk and thirty men. Was it while General Leslie's troops were there that the Iona books were found and destroyed, having survived so much over so many centuries?

Covenanting zeal – or the boredom of thirty men garrisoned on a rocky outcrop in a hostile sea – may well have brought an end to the remnants of the Iona library.

MacLean of Duart then tried to take the castle back, and this was the start of a long and bloody conflict, which, for the Iona books, if they were still extant, could have been a catastrophic period. The intricacies of the Civil Wars in Scotland involved not only religion but the settling of spats between individuals. The 9th Earl of Argyll found himself in dire financial straits because of the ongoing politicking surrounding the Stuart kings, and he went after his debtors to try to regain some of his family's lost wealth. Entries in the 9th Earl's diary for 11–19 July 1679 describe skirmishes around the Cairnburgh islands which left them still in the hands of the MacLeans and the earl no better off. Some four decades later, while the Stuarts were still attempting to regain the throne, Cairnburgh was held alternately by MacLeans and government forces during the 1715 Uprising. The government gained the upper hand and garrisoned the castle on a permanent basis. The plan of the islands drawn up by Robert Johnson in 1741 shows the defences of the day, but in the event – the Uprising of 1745 – no attempt was made on the castle.

If the manuscripts survived all that, could they still be present on the islands today? Certainly, when a group from St Andrews University Archaeology Society carried out a dig on the Treshnish Isles in the 1950s to look for the lost books of Livy, they found nothing. But it is not yet time to write off this curious possibility. Sarah Moore of the Hebridean Trust informs this author that preparations for a new dig are now under way. The lost books may yet see the light of day.

8
SEPULCHRAL STATEMENTS

Funerary monuments may be informative. They may be beautiful. They may blaze abroad the wealth and power of the deceased, give clues to his occupation, or reveal the poverty in which he died. Argyll is full of such markers, grave slabs and headstones. The most ancient are the impressive communal cairns of the pre-Christian era. Then came the carved crosses that marked individual graves in Columban times; but as individual status increased in importance, more personalised slabs and headstones came into use. Some date back to the Vikings, many to medieval times, and the eighteenth and nineteenth centuries abound with gravestones which mark not only the death of a man, woman or child but the death of a settlement. The amateur historian Allan Begg spent many years using the placenames on headstones in Mid Argyll to trace lost villages which had crumbled away after the evictions of the nineteenth century, or, by the latter end of the twentieth century, had been swallowed up in forestry plantations.

The Celtic schools of carving on Iona, and at Loch Sween, Loch Awe, Saddell and elsewhere, left a tracery of flora and fauna across great slabs of stone commemorating the dead. Swords of state, suits of armour and prancing horses on grave slabs from Ardnamurchan to Kintyre contrast with the sobering lists of dead child after dead child – during the eighteenth century in Kilbrandon and Kilchattan parish in the Presbytery of Lorn, many babies born to quarriers' wives died of lockjaw before they reached eight days old. In Knapdale, sad roll calls are carved to remember eight or nine children dead before the age of ten, several bearing the same name in the melancholy hope that one Morag, Alasdair or Iain would survive to carry on a family name. Latin inscriptions (*Hic jacet*: 'Here lies') such as those at Kilberry, Kilmichael, Kilmartin and Kilneuair remind us of those who were leaders of men. In Kintyre, at Kilchousland, Killean and at Clachan, precisely carved ploughing teams and fishing boats commemorate those who worked on land and at sea in the eighteenth century.

Medieval grave slab for an Argyll knight.

There is only one grave in Argyll, however, which uses not just one stone but many to mark a man's passing and catalogue all of the prejudices he held in life. On the island of Luing, near neighbour of Belnahua and a slate island belonging to the Breadalbane Estate, Alexander Campbell lies in a grave in the ancient churchyard of Kilchattan; it is hard to think of him being at rest. The slate quarried from the island is also used to mark the graves there, and Alexander Campbell, self-styled Covenanter, prepared a number of them before his death on 4 November 1829, as well as digging his own grave. Only the date of his death had to be inserted after he had breathed his last. Well prepared and leaving nothing to chance, he wanted posterity to know what he thought of his fellow man, having left his contemporaries in no doubt while he was living.

Curious as the presence of this plethora of brimstone-breathing commemorative stones may be, it is perhaps still more curious that they were given the space Campbell demanded for them. The Rev. John Macfarlane, the minister of 'Killbrandon and Killchattan', who wrote the first statistical account of the parish, published in the 1790s, reported that all 2,060 inhabitants were Protestants and that the few 'sectaries' among them 'call themselves Covenanters'. By 1836, the parish had lost the

A grave in Clachan churchyard, Kintyre, which commemorates an eighteenth-century ploughman. *Crown Copyright © Royal Commission on the Ancient and Historical Monuments of Scotland.*

double 'l's from its name but gained 200 dissenters, 'chiefly Covenanters and Independents', according to the *Statistical Account* of 1834–45. This was just a few years after Alexander Campbell's death and there is little doubt that he was responsible for this dramatic increase in the parish, which had taken place in less than four decades.

Campbell's brand of Covenanting was not that of the men and women of religious principle and Scottish patriotism who were the first Covenanters in the seventeenth century. A Reformed Church was established in Scotland in 1561 which was separated not only from what was seen to be a corrupt Church of Rome, but also from the interference of the state. When, in 1603, the Scottish and English crowns were united and James VI of Scotland also became James I of England, there were fears for the status of that new Church. These grew on the accession of Charles I in 1625 and developed into open alarm when his coronation was held in Edinburgh in 1633. Many Scots were determined that Charles, a man with very High Church leanings, would not impose himself as head of the democratic, self-governing Presbyterian Church.

In Argyll, Archibald Campbell, Lord Lorn, eldest son of the 7th Earl, heir to the chiefdom of the clan into which Alexander had been born a lowly member, had been put in charge of the estates when his father had renounced Protestantism and gone off to fight for Philip III of Spain. He was made a privy councillor in 1628, and two years after Charles I's enthronement in Edinburgh he succeeded to the title as 8th Earl of Argyll and was considered to be the most powerful figure in Scotland. Charles had already sought and received the reluctant support of the earl for his insistence on the premise of the divine right of kings, but in 1637 he moved to reintroduce bishops and a prayer book to Scotland. The General Assembly of the Church of Scotland had not been consulted and its members were outraged. So was the new earl, not least because Charles, while to his face currying favour on the religious front, had gone behind his back to ask the Earl of Antrim to invade Argyll and incite the MacDonalds against him.

Using the 1581 'King's Confession' document, which required the king as well as the people to maintain the Reformed Church in Scotland, a National Covenant was drawn up which again demanded that there would be neither interference from the king nor any reintroduction of 'Papistry'. Scotland's people wanted no intermediaries between them and God and 300,000 'covenanted' or signed this document, led by the Earl of Argyll. Argyll then took both military and civil action against the king and his supporters.

Charles, of course, retaliated and so began those bloody decades of civil war. In England, he threw out parliament, and, after an eleven-year dictatorship, was himself thrown out by the Puritans. The Puritans sought the support of the Presbyterians in Scotland, who saw the opportunity to negotiate for a Reformed Church south of the Border. In 1646, Charles surrendered to the Scottish Covenanter army, which handed him over to the English parliament. The parliament not only executed the king; it reneged on the religious part of the deal to reform the Church of England and separate it from the State.

It was as hideous as all such conflicts are hideous, but politically and in religious terms, the demands which thousands of Scots had made in the National Covenant for a free Scottish parliament and a free General Assembly were hugely significant, both in 1638 and into the future. They were potent enough to inspire men like Alexander Campbell 150 years later, when he became leader of a secession from the recognised

Presbyterian Church in 1787. There may have been a whiff of romanticism in his following the footsteps of the seventeenth-century clan chief, but Alexander Campbell and his fellow Cameronians, Covenanters or Remonstrants, as the seceders were variously known, were convinced that they alone were of the one true and very narrowly defined faith – an uncompromising faith which believed all outside of itself damned.

The secession in Lorn came about because of the arrival of a new minister who was seen as an 'Erastian' – believing, as the Swiss theologian Thomas Erastus had done in the sixteenth century, that the State should have authority over the Church. Alexander Campbell led a handful of like-minded believers off to form their own congregation, and these latter-day Covenanters were, because of Campbell's leadership, mainly centred on the island of Luing. By the 1840s that congregation had grown to 200 within the parish of Kilbrandon and Kilchattan. Exclusive, bitter and intolerant, even Campbell's bleak charisma could not hold it together and it eventually imploded because its members couldn't agree.

If Alexander Campbell's self-scribed memorial tablets – and the digging of his own grave – could suggest that in his dying days he was, in modern parlance, 'disturbed', his own testimony does not indicate a happy or normal childhood. In his 'Dying Testimony' he remembered

Kilchattan chapel had a long history, but by the late eighteenth century the New Covenanters had broken with the Prebyterian parish. *A. Scott Rankin.*

himself as a child who did not like to play, was not tempted by other children to play on the Sabbath, and was mocked by them for his sanctimony. 'Put on the preaching eyes now', they'd demand – was he bullied into looking pious or did he revel in the notice he received? His attention-grabbing series of gravestones and memorials might suggest the latter. Although he was born in 1751, just five years after the defeat of the Catholic Prince Charles Edward Stuart at Culloden, it is difficult to know what influences impinged on the world of a child on the island of Luing. Lorn was not an area where people supported the Pretender and so there was no retribution to contend with. But all coastal settlements are privy to news from elsewhere, and the sailors who bring the news also transmit the tensions and prejudices of the day. Isolated though they were, the people of Luing would have heard of the way other Highlanders and Islanders had been treated and of the great political and religious debates unfolding in more populous areas.

Whatever was happening elsewhere, Luing and the Slate Islands were a small, formidable and introverted Gaelic-speaking world of slate quarrying, fishing and farming. Like many islands off Scotland's west coast, Luing could be a sunny welcoming paradise – or a bleak, inhospitable place swept by strong winds for two-thirds of the year, as the *First Statistical Account* records. The southern end of the island is fertile and today Luing is famous for the pedigree cattle developed by the Cadzow family. The villages of Toberonochy on the east coast, and Mill Bay and Cullipool on the west were created to house the quarriers. Now invitingly picturesque, in their era as workers' cottages they would have been as grim as the basic housing in any Lanarkshire mining village.

Slate quarrying had begun at the end of the 1600s when men would have done anything to put food in the bellies of their families: not only was Scotland beggared by the previous decades of conflict, there were also what Martin Martin called 'the years of scarcity', when bitter winters and sodden summers led to failed crops and starvation. The poor became tied into the slate industry, and a hundred years later one man in three worked in the quarries. Around 5 million slates were quarried each year and the annual wage bill was £4,000. The day labourers were paid 9 or 10 pence a day – less than 5 modern pence. There was always a shortage of fuel, there was a tax on the ferries and the smithies, and all the farms were 'thirled' to a particular mill – obliged, in other words, to take their grain to a mill designated by the landlord and to accept the

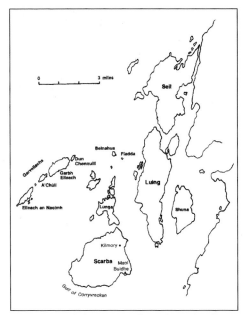

Luing and the surrounding slate islands.

conditions of payment there. Rheumatism was a constant companion in the damp climate and death was no stranger: too many babies died of infantile diseases; too many women died in childbirth; too many men lost their lives to the slate or the sea.

Perhaps it was not surprising, in such conditions, that there was dissent, and in a society where men could lose their jobs and their homes for speaking out against their employer or landlord – on Luing, that most usually amounted to the same thing – it was perhaps safer to rail against the Church. The minister in fact praised Breadalbane in the 1830s for providing rent-free cottages for the poor of the parish, but as his own living was granted by Breadalbane, he was unlikely to commit any criticism to paper, and, as we know from the *Oban Times*, fifty years later a descendant of Breadalbane was being mightily criticised for his hypocrisy in trying to combine Liberal politics with despotic employment methods.

Luing had never been easy for laymen or clergy. The patronage of the parish in early times went between the Dukes of Argyll and Breadalbane. In the 1670s and 1680s, the stance now taken by the Argyll family, of which the Breadalbanes were senior members, against the Catholic James VII and II, successor to the beheaded Charles, meant that ministers themselves had a hard time in Kilchattan. In 1685 the Rev. John Duncanson was charged with being in contempt of the king's authority. He was imprisoned at Campbeltown and died there on 29 September 1687. Kilchattan Chapel, which was first recorded in 1589 and is surrounded by the cemetery where Alexander Campbell is interred, then began to fall into disrepair and its roof finally fell in during 1745. When Campbell came here to dig his own grave, the Presbyterians were worshipping in a new church to the north and his band of Covenanters met at Ballachuan farm on the neighbouring slate island of Seil. Perhaps it is as well that he did not live later in the nineteenth century, when workers from Ballachulish came to work the slate at Cullipool and demanded the building of an Episcopalian church on Luing. He would indeed have believed the entire island to be damned.

Alexander Campbell was, of course, known by his Gaelic name, Alasdair Mac Iain Bhan. He lived at Achadanadure and he was seventy-eight years old when he died. His grave is not the only evidence of his presence in the old Kilchattan burial ground. Embedded in the wall outside the graveyard is a slate plaque which attempts to proselytise on behalf of the Covenanters. Another, placed above it, warns all against interfering with his memorial stones. Inside the walls, his headstone is a self-justifying self-testimony, and on the grave is a stone which reads, 'I protest that none be buried after me in this grave, which I have dug myself as Jacob did. Having adhered till death to the whole work of the Second Reformation in Scotland between year 1638 and 1649, and died in full assurance of the heavenly inheritance.'

While most are content to have our mere presence on this earth recorded on a headstone, perhaps embellished by a short epitaph, Campbell planned for some years the extent to which he could make use of his grave to get over his beliefs to a much wider audience than attended Covenanters' meetings. He was sure of his own 'election' – that he was one of those predestined to be in the presence of God. He believed in the 'pure Presbyterian religion, the covenanted cause of Christ and Church government'. He had, one stone assures us, adhered to 'the Confession of Faith, Second Reformation, purity and power of Covenants, and a noble Cloud of Witnesses that Jesus Christ is the head king and governor of the Church, and not mortal man as the king now is'.

He proclaimed on slate that 'The earth is the Lord's and not pope's earth, nor popish prelacy nor popish Erastianism either, this burial place

Alexander Campbell fulminated against all and sundry on the stones he cut for his own grave. *Rob Hunter.*

I testify that the earth is the Lord's also.' In stone he denounced the 'heinous sin of doctors and men for lifting the deads out of their graves before the Resurrection'. He appealed for popish monuments to be destroyed and that 'the Covenants be renued'.

There was much more in a closely written 'Dying Testimony', in which he denounced his own sect as well as King George III for his toleration of all denominations in Scotland, England and Ireland. He railed against those educated elsewhere than 'the college of Sina and Zion'; the grave robbers; play actors and pictures; women with veils and umbrellas; dancing schools; 'women that wear Babylonish garments, that are rigged out with stretched-out necks, tinkling as they go'; 'the low country, as they are not kind to strangers'; steamboats; modern corn dryers; and un-Christian beards.

His very lengthy fulmination included all the faiths he must ever have encountered or read of, headed by the Roman Catholics and Atheists but also including the Quakers, Anabaptists, Haldians, Arminians, Unitarians, Methodists, New Jerusalemites, Glassites and all sectarians. Little wonder that the Rev. Mr John Macfarlane, minister of Kilbrandon and Kilchattan, said of the Covenanters that their 'charity is not very extensive'.

The extent of Campbell's memorial stones and the length of his 'Dying Testimony' indicate that this was a man determined not to go unnoticed by posterity. He was ignored neither during his lifetime nor after his death. Today, some may see Luing as remote and cut off from the mainstream of life, but Alexander Campbell, born in 1751 and making trouble in the Church by his mid thirties, evoked comment from the most eminent religious figures in Scotland. In his lifetime, and perhaps more kindly than he would have himself phrased such criticism, Dr Somerville, a leader of the Reformed Presbyterians, said, 'Sandy is an honest man, but full of spiritual pride.' After Campbell's death, the man who would become Moderator of the Church of Scotland in 1877, Dr K. M. Phin, said, 'What Luther was to the Reformation, that was he to the Free Secession in a wide district of the Highlands.' Such comparison with one of the most influential names in the history of the Christian Church would surely have gratified Alexander Campbell, that man 'full of spiritual pride'. This hint at the breadth of his influence also gives a clue to the origins of his curious knowledge of parasols and play actors, veils and long whiskers, dancing schools and tinkling jewellery. His

Even the wall outside the ancient chapel bears witness to the bitterness of the 'New Covenanter'. Here, Campbell warns that if any meddle with the stone, the judgement executed on King Jehoiakim would also befall them, as related in Psalm 140. *Rob Hunter.*

View from the windswept hillside where Alexander Campbell lies,
probably less than peacefully. *Rob Hunter.*

gravestones may lie on a windswept island hillside, but this was a man
who went out into the world to preach his Covenanting beliefs – and
found the world sadly wanting.

9

CAVES AND CURSES

Cowal is just a stone's throw from the end of Scotland's industrial belt. It is a comfortable commuter distance from the peninsula to Glasgow and 'twas ever thus: the kings of Scotland, using Dumbarton Castle as a stepping stone in the days when Glasgow was nothing more than a dear green place, could always find time to cross the Clyde to this beautiful corner of Argyll. And yet, for all its nearness to the heart of power and modernity, this peninsula maintains a curious link to the primitive, the forces of nature and the supernatural.

In Argyll, modern technology is frequently attacked by the elements: computers go into meltdown, cashline machines are disabled, petrol pumps cannot dispense fuel. Scientists say lightning is the cause. Argyll roads and harbours flood frequently, and tinkling burns are turned into raging, destructive torrents in minutes. Scientists say this is another symptom of global warming. Some people, however, retain a sneaking belief that these violent meteorological exhibitions are evidence that Cailleach Bheir, the Old Woman of the Thunderbolt, is still at work in her numerous hilltop homes. And when adventurous cavers, seeking new depths as Munro-baggers seek new heights, venture deep into the interiors of the many cavernous grottoes which the peninsula has to offer, whose spirit might they encounter?

Even a man of the cloth wondered in as sober a publication as the *First Statistical Account*, 1791, whether 'the Cailleach' had had a hand in what might have been a great human tragedy and was an agricultural and economic disaster. The Rev. Charles Stewart, minister in the parishes of Strachur and Stralachlan, reported that in the autumn of 1780 a mudslide in the hills to the north-east of Loch Eck had destroyed around ten acres of good arable land and eight houses. Because the phenomenon, caused by what Mr Stewart described as 'a remarkable water spout' which fell on part of the parish, occurred around 2 o'clock in the afternoon, the inhabitants of the houses were either out working or heard the commotion and were able to run out of the way of the mudslide. Men who tried to save their belongings from their houses found themselves in great danger and had to give up on their mission.

The rocks and debris which came down the hillside made the job of clearing the area prohibitively expensive. The parish stepped in to help the poorest crofters and Mr Stewart reported that the 'landlord behaved with the greatest humanity to the tenants'.

The disaster was nothing new. Just a few years previously, the dwellings on a farm to the north-west of Loch Eck had been swept away by a similar deluge, which caused Mr Stewart, no doubt a well-educated man with a firm belief in his God, to again suggest the work of 'Cailleach-vear'. This powerful old woman was – is – not confined to Stralachlan, where she is said to live and keep her herds of cows around the confines of a huge stone on the ridge which separates Stralachlan from Glendaruel. She is a woman of many homes, all in the high mountains, such as Beinn a' Bheithir to the east of Kentallen in Appin – the Ben of the Thunderbolt. Her powers are mightier than any humanly engineered force of water, and it is she who was responsible for the very presence of Loch Awe, Loch Eck, and many other immense stretches of water.

In Stralachlan, or Strathlachlan as it is spelled today, Mr Stewart was bold enough to suggest that superstition and ignorance offer answers to questions which could be answered by meteorology and geophysics. The forces of nature in these parts contain such power that an uneducated people would quite naturally see in them supernatural forces seeking appeasement. Where the Cailleach Bheir is said to live in Strathlachlan is a place in which thunder becomes trapped and rumbles around angrily for hour after hour; the water which tumbles down the hillsides after a storm could convince anyone that Loch Eck was once a fertile valley and that the Old Woman of the Thunderbolt flooded it in a fit of temper. It would be easy enough to believe that her herds of cattle are augmented by those she steals from local farmers at the height of one of her furious barrages.

The Cailleach has more than one home on the peninsula itself. To the west of Glendaruel and overshadowing the River Ruel at Conchra is Cailleach a' Bheathrach, another summit named after the Old Woman of the Thunderbolt. To the north of Castle Lachlan, further up the peninsula, a lower hill is said to be the home of a witch who answers to a whistle – but beware. The Argyll historian, author and amateur archaeologist Marion

Campbell of Kilberry, whistled up the witch from Crarae Gardens on the opposite side of Loch Fyne as an experiment in the presence of a witness and together they suddenly found themselves under darkened skies with a wind howling about their ears. It does not pay to meddle with those who can bring down a curse in the time it takes to say 'cailleach'. Weather is not just weather in Argyll: the minister of Lochgoilhead and Kilmorich said in the 1834–45 *Statistical Account* that the 'face of the Heavens is generally louring and cloudy', that rain was heavy and frequent, that the winds 'rush through the glens with irresistible violence', and that the 'transitions of heat and cold are sudden and violent'. The Old Woman of the Thunderbolt had much to answer for.

Bera – or Vear as Mr Stewart called her – was an important personage and not to be trifled with. According to Ossian, the third-century Irish bard, she lived in the cave of the rock and was the daughter of Gripian the Sage. Hers was a respected family but she was last in line. She had been left in charge of a spring, which each evening before the sun went down she had to cover with a special stone carved with sacred symbols. One hot day she fell asleep in the sunshine and didn't wake in time to

Cowal is riddled with caves, some accessible like this one, other hidden from view and tunnelling deep into the hillsides. *Ivan Young.*

cover the spring before the sun set. All the waters of the mountain burst out and drowned the beautiful, fertile plain below, along with all the cattle which grazed there. This was the creation of Loch Awe – or any other lough or loch to which it seemed most appropriate to attribute the legend. When Bera saw what she had done, she shrieked in anguish. The mountain – in this case we must assume Ben Cruachan – shook from its base. Bera's spirit retired to be among the ghosts of her fathers in what Ossian described as 'their light and airy halls'.

Were these halls the caves which have provided shelter for paupers and the papers of earls down the centuries since Bera returned to her ancestors? Argyll is a county riddled with caves, but some parts of the Cowal peninsula resemble a Swiss cheese, and some remarkable caves have become part of today's leisure industry. Once, however, they served very different purposes. Around 7000 BC, it is likely that the nomads who came to Bute and Cowal made use of the many caves in the area. When the princes of Antrim invaded in the fourth century AD and Comhghall was granted the running of the peninsula, the caves must have presented welcome hideouts for those under attack. When the Vikings were fighting to maintain their presence in Scotland in the early twelfth century and lost so drastically that Glenduisk, 'glen of black water', became Glen-da-ruail, 'glen of red blood', the caves would have again provided safe places in which to hide vulnerable women and children, cattle and possessions. It was a pattern to be repeated for many centuries to come.

In the parish of Strachur and Stralachlan, the Rev. Charles Stewart listed a number of large caves in his 1791 report. These included Uamhachorolaich, 'the strange fellow's cave', on the farm of Balliemor, where the said strange fellow took his wife and children to live. He then 'preyed on the neighbourhood at night'. Perhaps the man had a mental health problem, or perhaps he was simply so poor that this was the only way he could keep his family alive. In 1783 there was a population of 1,061 in the joint parish, all attempting to live off poor soil and the fishing. It was in this parish within the next decade that Donald Maclachlan of Maclachlan, 'under necessity of thinning the population' on a number of his farms, would create a village – now known as Newton – for twelve of his poorest cottars and provide them with two fishing boats on condition that they would pay him back 'from the produce of their industry'. Raising sheep for mutton and wool, and timber for the iron-ore smelter at Furnace on the other side of Loch Fyne were much more profitable than any arable farming of the poor, thin soil of the parish. Poverty perhaps came too soon to the man who retreated with his family to the cave at Balliemor. Had he hung on a decade or so he might have been offered a two-roomed cottage and a share in a fishing boat at Newton – but then MacLachlan of MacLachlan left things a little late himself. The herring bonanza which had brought up to six hundred boats a night into Loch Fyne in the 1700s dwindled drastically in the nineteenth century.

Some caves did not offer a welcome: one in the side of Tur-na'n Calman, 'Fort of the Doves', created a noise which the minister graphically described as sounding like stones rolling over 'sheets of copper'. Others were commodious enough to hold scores of men. Carnach Mhor could, according to Mr Stewart, hold fifty armed men standing easily, and it opened up into several linked 'apartments'. Modern explorers of these caves say they are not quite so commodious as the eighteenth-century descriptions suggest, but are impressively large nonetheless.

In the neighbouring parish of Lochgoilhead and Kilmorich the caves are equally capacious. One, which has an entrance just 4 feet high opening into a cavern 70 feet in circumference and 10 feet high, was described by the minister in 1840 as having cellars leading off it and a narrow passage leading to a smaller 'apartment'.

In a remarkable letter written to 'all the native men, vassals and good Tenants dwelling on the lands of Ardkinglas both men and women' at Christmas in 1905, Niall Diarmid Campbell, laird and 'curator of Ardkinglas', recounts the family's history back to medieval times. In sharing the fortunes of their clan chiefs, the earls of Argyll, the Ardkinglas Campbells found themselves in flight on more than one occasion, and, in fleeing, at least one took to the Cowal caves.

In the early years of the British Civil Wars, Sir James Campbell, the 9th Laird, supported the 8th Earl of Argyll. As Niall Diarmid Campbell wrote a century ago his ancestor's life was 'one long record of tumultuous war, raid and foray'. Miraculously, in 1645 Sir James was one of the few who escaped from Inverlochy, while 40 Campbell lairds lay slain. The following year he was defeated by the men of Atholl and the Laird of Inchbrakie at the Battle of Callander, where he led 1,200 of his own men. A decade later, Sir James Lamont of Inveryne came after him for his treatment of Lamont followers, and in 1654 Sir James Campbell was cited before the Privy Council for murdering many of the Lamont clan.

After being indicted for murder in 1661, he escaped and was declared a fugitive and a traitor in an elaborate ceremony at the Market Cross in Edinburgh in which his coat of arms was fixed backwards to the cross and then torn publicly to the sound of trumpets.

Unlike his clan chief, the Ardkinglas laird was never restored to his barony, but his eldest son, Iain, had the family lands and titles restored by the intervention of the 9th Earl of Argyll in 1665. Charles II made him a baronet in 1669 and all seemed to be back on course; but the years of bloodshed were not over, and, as the young Ardkinglas had tied his colours to the mast of the 9th Earl, there were great troubles ahead. When the earl became involved in the plot to depose James II and install William of Orange on the British throne, Ardkinglas became part of the support waiting in Argyll to set the revolution in motion. As we shall see, this was not to be: instead Ardkinglas Castle, along with Carrick and Inveraray, were seized by the Marquess of Atholl's men. Iain fled to the hills and hid in one of the immense caves in the area, now known as Uamh-vic-Iain Riabhaich, a name which translates as the 'Cave of Grizzled John'. The experience of living in a cave, however commodious and however safe, might well have turned Iain Campbell grey. It proved a safe enough hiding place to which the laird's faithful tenants could bring all his provisions without him being detected for a whole year, according to Niall Campbell's letter to the tenants of 1905, and this story also appears in the *Statistical Account* of 1791, written soon enough after the event to have been passed on by the families who fought for and then provided for their laird.

His tale did not have the same unfortunate outcome that, as we shall see, befell the clan chief. After this curious interlude in his lair in the hills, Ardkinglas was captured and imprisoned at Blackness Castle and then taken on to Edinburgh Castle in 1685. In the strange political climate of the day, he managed to escape execution, and when he was eventually liberated, he became the MP for Argyll, as well as sheriff and justice depute – possibly the first and last time in British history that a troglodyte has sat in parliament.

It is curious enough that a laird should spend a year in a cave, but it was a custom of the area to flee to the caves when plunderers came and for plunder to be hidden in them. One labyrinth in these honeycombed hills is actually called Uamh na Plunderain. The system is entered from a narrow passage which opens first into a small underground apartment and then, with the help of a ladder, into another which is 12 feet high. A third apartment is a veritable hall, 24 feet long, 15 feet wide and 15 feet high. Although the stalagmites indicate water once ran freely, the bottom of the cave is dry as a bone. Beyond this again is another room of the same dimensions as the first. In recent years a copper plate with its name in Gaelic and English was fastened to a rock at the entrance to the first cave, but no doubt there was no 'nameplate' on the door in times gone by, because this and many caves like it were the shelter of either the attackers or the attacked.

Archibald Campbell, the 9th Earl, had succeeded his father to the title in 1663 under difficult circumstances. There had been a delay, because although he did not share the 8th Earl and First Marquess's politics, the fact that the Covenanting Marquess had been executed for treason in Edinburgh in 1661 meant his son was considered with suspicion. As Lord Lorn, the 9th Earl had committed himself to the Royalist cause, taking a leading role in the Glencairn Rising in the 1650s against Oliver Cromwell's forces, but a king – and the father who had opposed that king's claim to divine right over Church and State – had been executed since then, and now that the monarchy had been restored no one was taking any chances. Campbell's main enemy was the Earl of Middleton, Charles II's right-hand man in Scotland – an ambitious fellow who sought to rectify his own lack of territory by seizing Argyll's. He set out to destroy the Argyll heir and made use of a letter intercepted at the beginning of the 1660s to accuse Lorn of attempting to stir up dissension against the new king. It was a capital offence and he was found guilty in August 1662; but the king himself said the sentence should not be carried out. The meddlesome Middleton soon brought about his own downfall, and Lorn was released from prison in Edinburgh in June 1663 and created 9th Earl of Argyll. The title of marquess was, however, stripped from the family.

A young man in his early thirties, the new earl was admitted to the Privy Council, but he was no longer wealthy enough to wield the power his father had. There were heavy debts to be repaid and many of the properties acquired by his father during his Covenanting days were returned to their rightful owners. Like the servant in the Bible who, given time by a generous landlord to pay his own debts, rushed off and throttled the money he was owed out of men poorer than himself, the new earl went after MacLean of Duart on Mull, his major debtor. His war with the MacLeans during the 1670s rocked the already unstable Highlands and also gave ammunition to his enemies in parliament who wanted to strip him of the Argyll title – or worse. It was suggested that the son of a traitor was attempting to wipe out one of the most loyal clans.

While this clan feuding to restore the Argyll fortunes raged, another drama was unfolding. Charles II did not have a legitimate heir. His brother James had converted to Catholicism and it looked as if he would be the next king. In England, a plot against James was revealed in 1678. There were even moves to make Charles's illegitimate son, the Duke of Monmouth, his legal heir. In a move calculated to bring Scottish nobles on board to support his succession, James went to Scotland and introduced a Test Bill in 1681 which demanded an oath swearing support not only for royal authority over state and Church, but also for an heir deemed legitimate by Charles II, whatever that heir's religion. Instead, the Lord President of the Court of Session suggested reverting to the 1560 Confession of Faith, which had been ratified by the court of James VI of Scotland in 1567. This said that the only head of the Church could be Lord Jesus and there could be no form of Church government except Presbyterianism and urged the faithful to resist tyranny. The resulting Test was a muddle which demanded conflicting convictions from those who swore to it.

Many refused to take this new oath. Argyll swore, but boxed clever by adding his own clause that the oath had to be consistent with the Protestant religion. Perhaps glad that one leading figure in Scotland was prepared to conform in some way to his wishes, James allowed this – but Argyll's enemies didn't. They wanted him to be tried for treason for this twisting of the oath and they succeeded. Not certain that the royal household would be as clement as it claimed it would be, Argyll escaped from Edinburgh Castle. Curiously, considering his own previous antagonism towards the Covenanters his father had led, it was with the help of Covenanters and former New Model Army officers that he fled south and hid uneasily in London. He had lost the Argyll fortunes again and, ignominiously, had been helped by those he had opposed in his youth.

When Charles died in 1685, the Catholic James did indeed come to the throne and plots against him were two a penny. In Amsterdam and Rotterdam, where the exiles who had opposed the Stuarts from the outset had congregated, schemes were hatched to depose James and put the Protestant William of Orange on the throne. The 9th Earl of Argyll found himself not just in the thick of this ferment, but suddenly at its head. He raised money and arms and was sure that the Campbells would rise up behind him if he invaded Scotland on behalf of William. Some caution entered into the scheme when Argyll's Scottish colleagues became worried that he was wielding too much power: he was told to take action only after consultation with the Scottish council. Argyll's self-seeking was not the major problem, however. As Charles Edward Stewart was to discover some sixty years later, co-ordination is of the essence, and the plan was for co-ordination between the earl in Scotland and the Duke of Monmouth in England in mounting a two-pronged attack on behalf of William of Orange. That co-ordination was sadly lacking.

Argyll sailed to the west of Scotland via the Orkneys and found that few Campbells were free, willing, or able to follow his standard. In Campbeltown, men did join the mission, and with the promise of 1,200 men at Tarbert it was decided to meet there. Argyll had brought a portable printing press with him to recruit support: in the event, the pamphlets would only serve to condemn him.

Atholl was waiting for his arrival, having been ordered to 'destroy all houses, goods and persons of any who join with Argyll'. As the Laird of Ardkinglas had already discovered, Atholl was taking these orders literally. Innocent men, women and children, implicated for no better reason than that the men on whose estates they lived were considered to be traitorous enemies, found themselves suffering savage retribution at the hands of Atholl's men. The massive caves around Lochgoilhead were the sanctuary not only of a laird, but of many innocent fugitives from the parish. There were a thousand or so people living in the parish, and many, along with their possessions, were safely – even comfortably – hidden away. From their shelter they were able to make successful surprise attacks on the Men of Atholl. But, as the Lochgoilhead and Kilmorich minister pointed out in the 1791 *Statistical Account*, nothing could stop the houses from being burned or the cattle from being stolen or slaughtered.

Atholl was also commanded to execute all heritors and 'a hundred of the ringleaders among the tenants and commoners'. In the face of such rigourous depredations, even the caverns of Cowal were not safe for the scores who sought to hide in them, and many were caught, tortured and imprisoned, or transported to the New World.

Rothesay Castle was destroyed by Argyll's own men in the chaos of the 1685 attempt to put James VII and II off the throne. *Argyll and Bute Library Service.*

In all this confusion and indecision, the Earl of Argyll crossed from Kintyre to Bute, where Cromwell's forces had left the castle in a very poor state in 1659, and then into the Cowal peninsula. He wanted, of course, to make an attempt on his own headquarters at Inveraray, and he headed there up through Glendaruel to Ardkinglas, where he took the castle back from Atholl's men. Inveraray Castle, however, was now very firmly held by the Royalists and he had to turn back. In fact, he had little choice as his men were deserting in great numbers. Castle Carrick, where the family's appointed constable had for centuries guarded estate documents, had been captured by government forces and destroyed. At the hands of Argyll's own men, Rothesay Castle suffered another blaze in a battle against government forces. The castle on Eilean Dearg ('Red Island') in the Kyles of Bute became the Earl's main arsenal, in the vain hope that the narrow entrance into Loch Riddon would prevent its notice by the government ships. He was also keeping prisoners there and had a garrison of 180 men guarding cannon, muskets and gunpowder. Suddenly, the forces who under a Captain Hamilton had destroyed Carrick Castle now moved in on the little island with a fire ship. Argyll's garrison fled to save themselves, setting a fuse to the powder magazine and leaving the prisoners to be blown with the castle to kingdom come. The prisoners, however, waved 'a whyte cloutt' and Captain Hamilton's

Carrick Castle, once a depository for the Earls of Argyll's precious
papers, was destroyed in 1685 by government forces.

men were alerted to the situation. They moved the weaponry and the
prisoners out and then blew up the castle themselves. The game was up
for the 9th Earl. As he attempted to escape to the south with one of his
soldiers, a Major Fullarton, he was seized at Inchinnan on 18 June 1685
by the local militia. It is said that a drunken weaver named John Riddell
hit the earl on the head with a sword.

He was taken to Edinburgh and a week later was beheaded, just
as his father had been. The Duke of Monmouth died at the Battle of
Sedgemoor on 6 July, wiping out the two prongs of the 1685 rebellion.
Ironically, if the two of them had left James to his own devices, they
could have kept their lives and seen him ousted more peacefully and
legitimately as a result of his excesses just three years later.

When the executed earl's son, now the 10th Earl of Argyll, was presented to the new king and queen, William and Mary, he was not as
impoverished as might have been expected. Despite the disasters of 1685,
the bloody battles around Inveraray and throughout the 9th Earl's territories in southern Argyll, and the final iniquity of the execution, Argyll had
in one sense kept his head. The castle at Inveraray may have been held by
his enemies, but his friends had already taken all the most valuable documents – the charters and titles of the Argyll Estates – across Loch Fyne and
down Lock Eck to be secreted in what became known as the Paper Cave.

In his *Chronicles of Cowal*, Angus McLean suggests that Argyll papers were hidden in this cave three times during the period when Inveraray was sacked time and again. Certainly the castle was in no state for man nor papers by the end of these conflicts. In earlier times, when birlinns were the peak of naval might, Carrick Castle might have offered an alternative, but it was exposed to attack at the mouth of Loch Goil and the more sophisticated and powerfully armed seventeenth-century English naval vessels had no trouble in causing it terminal damage. An inaccessible cave was a better option than any besieged castle.

The Paper Cave, around 12 miles south of Inveraray, sits on Clach Beinn, in the heart of traditional Campbell country. Clach Beinn is 2,107 feet high and joins to Beinn Mhor, over 300 feet higher, via the horseshoe of a high corrie. The cave itself is some 560 feet above Loch Eck, opposite the Coylet Inn on the loch shore, a coaching hostelry which the earl would have been familiar with and which survives to this day. The area had been a deer park for centuries and was wooded with oak, birch and alder. The Paper Cave is a deep one and the ideal place for the precious charters of the Argylls. The superstitious of the seventeenth century may have claimed that the rockfalls which formed the cave had been instigated by Cailleach Bera throwing some of her thunderbolts, but in a report written for the *Grampian Speleological Group Bulletin* in January 1980 Jackie Yuill gives the modern scientific cause

High above Coylet Inn, a coaching inn even in the 9th Earl of Argyll's day, lies the Paper Cave, in which the family documents were hidden. *Argyll and Bute Library Service.*

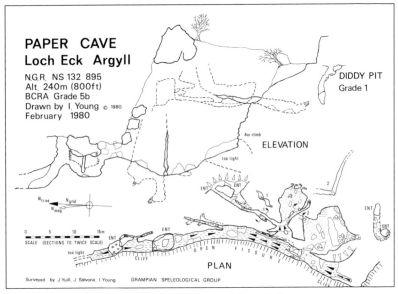

Paper Cave. *Grampian Speleological Group.*

for such a cave's existence. This whole area is just north of that curious natural frontier known as the Highland Boundary Fault, and because of the great stresses experienced by the Earth's crust here Beinn Mhor and Clach Beinn are the site of many massive landslips and deep rifts. A massive flake of white mica which has split from the main rift at an angle of 90 degrees forms the Paper Cave The roof of the cave, which is about 8 metres square, is unbroken micaschist and the floor is formed from shell-shaped slabs which have fallen from the roof. Yuill pointed out that despite this being an area where the annual rainfall averages over 200 centimetres, the low chamber formed by the rocks is very dry – an ideal place for a wooden chest containing the Argyll documents. But not only was the cave dry, it was also difficult to spot and difficult to penetrate. Ivan Young, who has photographed the cave, describes low chambers, some just a couple of feet high. Passages link the chambers, some sloping, some blocked, others lit through cracks in the rocks.

The Paper Cave may provide an interesting day out for members of a speleological group, and, given caving skills and permission from the Argyll Forest Park authorities, it is an exciting twenty-first-century expedition. Its position and its complexity were not a source of sporting challenge in the last decades of the seventeenth century, however: they

Inside the Paper Cave. *Ivan Young.*

were essential to the survival of one of Scotland's leading houses which was facing collapse. The 9th Earl of Argyll cannot have been the first in his line to use this as a place of concealment, but it is difficult to conceive of a cache of quite such importance ever having been secreted within the low-ceilinged chambers before this last act of a threatened chieftain. Such papers were essential proof of ownership at a time when registration of deeds was still in its infancy, and the earl no doubt had the future security of his family in mind even in those desperate last days. A faithful retainer is said to have been holed up on Island Farm off the shore of Lock Eck until it was safe to secrete the papers in the cave in 1685. He, or someone equally as faithful, made the return journey up the hillside to retrieve those papers and keep the House of Argyll afloat into a new century and a new political era.

The cave has been even more deeply hidden in recent times, deep in the Argyll forestry plantation. Should you wish to visit it, don't just seek permission from the Benmore Forest Office: make sure it is not a day when the Old Woman of the Thunderbolt is rattling her cutlery drawer.

10

A PLACE OF PILGRIMAGE

It was always a special place. A safe haven from the choppy waters of the Kilbrannon Sound and with enough natural protection to guard against possible enemies, it offered an invitation to the earliest settlers. They came here around 6000 BC, and they made weapons and tools to help them secure and develop their new home. As time passed, it became for a while the capital of the Dalriadic Kingdom. It was visited by men who would become saints, including the sixth-century Apostle of Kintyre, Ciaran – a man who also made use of Argyll caves and prayed in one on the shore of this sweeping bay. This was an ever-growing settlement which as the centuries rolled on became known first as Cill Chiaran ('Ciaran's Cell') and then as Ceann Loch Cille Chiaran ('Head of the Loch of Ciaran's Cell') In time, this was shortened and corrupted to Ceann Loch or Kinloch. Eventually, in 1700, it became the Royal Burgh of 'Campbeltoune'.

As can be imagined from the history of the House of Argyll in the 1600s, the fact that King William had first of all allowed Kinloch to be designated a free burgh of barony under the Campbells, and then to be called 'Campbeltoune' and given royal status must have seemed something of a miracle to the 10th Earl. Here was a man who could breathe a sigh of relief and feel safe to believe he would keep his head – rather than lose it, as his two predecessors had done.

The favoured position of Campbeltown brought prosperity. It was a good place for building ships, and for the import and export of goods, and in the eighteenth century the fishing from the Kilbrannon Sound north into Loch Fyne was something of a miracle for a population which often struggled to make a living. Although the soil was richer in Kintyre than further north in Argyll, this only served to allow the House of Argyll's 'plantations' of supporters from the neighbouring 'mainland' counties of Ayrshire and Renfrewshire to create a dairy industry with their imported milking cows and up-to-date farming methods. Fishing

Much herring was landed in Campbeltown's sheltered harbour
down the ages. *Maureen Bell.*

augmented incomes for the indigenous crofters. In the eighteenth century it wasn't just that the herring were suddenly more plentiful: the
quality of the fish was said by the minister of Saddell and Skipness, the
Rev. Mr George Macliesh, to be 'richer and more delicate of taste than
those caught either in the Western Isles or the coast of Ireland'. Fishing
boats went out in these waters in their hundreds, and the fleet which was
centred around Campbeltown was particularly successful.

In 1812, the world's first steamship, the *Comet,* was built on the
Clyde, and from the fairly modest task of transporting hotel guests
from Glasgow to Helensburgh it was soon speeding off to Loch Fyne,
Oban and even Fort William – although that was this particular boat's
downfall as the seas off the west coast proved too heavy for her. The
technology had been invented, however, and there was no stopping its
development. Bigger and better boats were made for the fishing and
nets became more sophisticated. In time, the catches were no longer
landed at Campbeltown, Tarbert and the smaller ports, but were delivered by the little fishing boats straight onto factory ships known as
'busses' which took the fish to the Clyde ports. Not only did the bigger
boats take the fish processing away from Loch Fyne: they were able to
pull in far greater hauls. The new ability to overfish greatly threatened
the industry in time.

However, the shoals of herring had always come and gone. In the 1640s, when the MacDonalds were wreaking vengeance on the Campbells throughout Argyll, many of the crofters whose homes and property were destroyed complained most bitterly if a boat had been burned, because the fishing that year was so good. Perhaps, then, the silver darlings were due to move off to other submarine pastures in the nineteenth century, but the advent of steam may well have speeded their departure.

As the fishing dwindled, however, the steamers created a new industry: tourism. Once the province of the wealthy, leisure travel was now possible for the 'ordinary' citizen and free time was spent visiting Dunoon, Rothesay, Tighnabruaich, Campbeltown, the Crinan Canal, Tarbert and Inveraray, courtesy of steamboats which allowed swift journeys in the wake of the royal birlinns of the past. The sailing jaunt undertaken by Queen Victoria and her consort Prince Albert in 1847, took in a visit to Inveraray Castle, which had been rebuilt along with the old dilapidated town in the 1740s, before a stately – some say Victoria thought boringly slow – progress through the Crinan Canal, spawned a million copycat journeys by the well-off and the less well-off, on private yachts and commercial steamers.

They came to Argyll to paint the scenery, to examine the wild flowers and to spot the birds – and, of course, in Victorian times that all too often meant taking their eggs for scholarly collections. There was a growing awareness of the long history of Argyll: amateur archaeologists were beginning to stumble over flints, standing stones, jet jewellery and Viking artefacts where none had been recognised less than a century before – in the 1791 *Statistical Account* the minister of Kilmartin, now considered one of the most important archaeological areas of Britain, wrote that there was nothing of note in his area.

Visitors may well have become acclimatised to the abundance of curiosities around Campbeltown and on into Kintyre and the rest of the county, but they would not have expected to find a miracle there. But 'miracle' was the first thought when a likeness of the figure of Christ crucified was discovered in August 1887, in a cave on Davaar Island, off the Campbeltown shore.

Someone purporting to have been in the party which discovered the figure wrote anonymously to the *Oban Times*, waxing lyrical. In the edition of 20 August he – or she – wrote, 'Daylight began to spread her pale grey tints above the eastern horizon, revealing a beautiful scene, as

Davaar Island presented a curiosity of the first order for a yachting
party in 1887.

our yacht approached Island Devaar [sic], that wave-like crested island at
the entrance of Campbeltown Loch.' The writer described the fishermen
bringing in the nets and 'thousands and thousands of herring struggling
in the brown nets and reflecting their silvery rays on the blue water'. The
group on the yacht had seen birds flying out from a cave on the island.
They noticed that it was a double cave and set out to explore 'all the
more minutely'. And, to their 'utmost astonishment', they saw the likeness of Christ crucified on the cave wall.

The party from the yacht were evidently a well-educated group of
people: they knew a painting when they saw one and were able to discuss its merits. One member 'suggested it was superior to Munkacsy's
Christ on Calvary', then on show in Paris. The painting was not easy
to see, but the group could make out that 'the muscles are the muscles
of an honest carpenter'. They saw that the painting was 15 feet across,
beginning about 8 feet above the bottom of the cave, and the figure was
about 7 feet high. The shape of the rock meant that the right hand was
invisible.

By the following week, the discovery had turned Davaar into a place
of pilgrimage. Some came in awe; some came to cast a critical eye. None
knew how the painting had been done or by whom. The editor sent
his own correspondent and reported: 'The inhabitants of Campbeltown

were suddenly converted into pilgrims on learning from last week's *Oban Times* that a discovery of the art painting, Christ Crucified, was made in a cave on the neighbouring Island of Davaar.' The tidal causeway to the island was lined with people of all ages heading to see the 'mysterious cave'. On the Sunday, the crowds were immense, swelled by visitors from far and wide. Art students came and, according to the *Oban Times*, 'passed their highest eulogiums on the unknown artist'.

These were the days of the 'fair' holidays. Glasgow, Paisley, Greenock and other industrialised towns took their turn for workers' holidays through July and early August. By mid August, schools were preparing for a new academic year and the fair weeks were coming to an end, yet every day of that week after the painting was discovered, the crowds grew. At first, it was 200-strong, heading for the island at low tide. By the end of the week, 1,200 were jostling to see this curious phenomenon: *Christ*

Christ on the Cross, by a mystery artist, was seen as a miracle by some. *Maureen Bell.*

on the Cross painted by an unknown artist. Between 4,000 and 5,000 pilgrims had made their way to Davaar, according to the *Oban Times*. The newspaper's reporter wrote that 'one pious person declared it to be a miracle from the Almighty', while another believed that 'an angel painted it'. Yet another theory put forward in the throng heading to the island was that St Kieran himself had been responsible for the painting. The Rev. Mr Rowson, an Episcopalian minister, then deceased, was said to have been seen visiting the cave daily – scarcely more fanciful than a suggestion that Munkacsy, the artist referred to by the intelligentsia in the yacht party which discovered the painting – 'was seen coming out of Mr MacFarlane's yacht during their visit to Campbeltown'. It was no more likely that the famous artist was secretly visiting the cave than that a dead minister had risen from the grave to carry out the work of art. The names of other well-known artists were put forward as the painter responsible, but a local wag told the journalist as they waited in line to see into the cave, 'Beware of Campbeltown, as the one half of the lies told in it are not true, and the other most certainly doubtful.'

And so, at the end of the first week, the artist was still unknown – and still revered. When he came forward and confessed to the act Archibald MacKinnon was suddenly seen by some as far less talented than the 'eulogiums' of the previous weeks had indicated. A prophet in his own country, this local artist and teacher was no longer praised by all for his *œuvre*.

Mr MacKinnon explained that he had wakened from a dream and felt compelled to paint the Crucifixion. He had seen in the dream the place where he should paint it and had gathered his paints and brushes together and at low tide crossed the narrow spit out to the island, painting in secret until it was done. But although he was criticised after his revelation, there were still those who wanted to see the 'miracle', and the local paper carried a report on 10 September that the crowds were still coming. Whatever sour grapes came his way, as the *Oban Times* pointed out, 'Mr MacKinnon, by his noble artistic effort and highly commendable conduct, has done more good to Campbeltown than anything we have yet heard of.'

In other words, business was booming because of the painting. Boat hirers, said to be 'almost in starvation' because of the economic climate, were making money hand over fist. Cobblers and shoemakers were busy, presumably because many failed to make the return journey from the

The caves on the southern side of Davaar, entered through cliff-high slashes in the rock, were a magnet to visitors from all over Britain and Europe.

island in time and got their feet badly wet. The grocers, bakers, butchers, newsagents, hoteliers, coach-hirers and steamboat companies were all basking in the warm economic glow generated by MacKinnon's curious painting.

And curious it was, that first naïve figure, necessarily foreshortened by the shape of the rocks. The first people to view it spoke of the honest muscles of the carpenter, but in fact MacKinnon had been compromised by his 'canvas' and possibly by the single shaft of light which allowed him to paint on it. Nonetheless, people wanted to see it, and they were advised by the newspapers that the ideal conditions under which to view were just after sunrise on a bright morning after a wet night. It is to be hoped that most put such romantic notions aside and instead opted to ask the times of the tides so that they could see it without getting their boots too wet.

As the weeks went by, artists and art critics came from all over Britain and 'even foreigners' made their way to Davaar to view; all were said to give approval. 'Splenetic jealousy' was afoot, however. There were those who charged MacKinnon with having copied a painting by Bonnat which had featured in the Paris Exhibition of 1878. Others made more mundane accusations: where had he got the paint? Hopefully not from the school. With such approbation ringing in his ears, MacKinnon packed up and left Campbeltown, leaving the pilgrims to gaze up at the life-size figure of Christ crucified and the cynics to sneer that Davaar Island had been 'pretty frequently visited in the past' and that no doubt the picture would provide an additional attraction.

Davaar is as iconic to the people of Campbeltown as Kisimul Castle is to the islanders of Barra or, indeed, McCaig's tower to the people of Oban – the first confirmation of home-coming, the last sight on leaving. At the northern, gently rounded end of the island is the lighthouse, while to the south, gaping in the jagged cliff face, is the MacKinnon cave. A volcanic plug, the island was quarried over a long period and its stone lies at the heart of Campbeltown – in houses, in the memorial to the war dead, in the very stones of the roads. There have been songs sung about it and poems written about it. Its presence makes Campbeltown what it is – a natural harbour waiting for man to build ships, to sail out to the fishing, to export to the world.

Quiet, polite, deferential Mr MacKinnon had boldly made his mark on this icon and changed it. A son of Campbeltown, born in 1857, he must have come from a fairly modest family because by the age of fourteen he was employed as a messenger boy in Glasgow. He had ambition however, and when he became apprenticed as an engineer, he went to evening classes at Glasgow School of Art. When he came home to Campbeltown, he became the art teacher at the local school. The mixed publicity which followed the discovery of his painting drove him away, and ironically, in order to leave he would have had to sail past the island and the painting in its cave as the roads through Kintyre were intermittent and dangerous in 1887.

He went to Liverpool and made use of his engineering apprenticeship by working at the Cammell Laird shipyard. He had married, and in time he and wife Mary and their daughter Dorothy, who was born in 1900, went to live at Nantwich in Cheshire. For a while, he worked as an itinerant artist, but eventually he was able to set up a studio in the town. Few of his paintings have survived, although there are civic canvases still to be seen in Nantwich. The first point-to-point race in the area was captured by him on canvas, and after the turn of the new millennium it sold for £250,000. Other MacKinnon canvases depicting scenes of Argyll

PICTURE CAVE, DAVAAR ISLAND, CAMPBELTOWN. A. 240

In 1934, MacKinnon returned to repaint his *Christ on the Cross*. It
was to be a completely different version. *Maureen Bell.*

have come up for auction on the Internet for several thousand pounds,
yet in his day his art did not succeed in the same way as did the works of
his contemporaries from Campbeltown, including William McTaggart,
grandfather of Sir William McTaggart.

He would never escape the painting which had come to him in a
dream: despite living so far from it, he would be involved with its maintenance to the end of his life, and it has gone on being of concern to the
art teachers of Campbeltown to this day. In 1902, two years after Dorothy was born, MacKinnon returned to Campbeltown to restore it. He
changed it then and again in 1934, when at the age of eighty-four he was
invited by the town council to come back home to maintain it.

Ronald Tognieri, called upon to restore the Davaar Island painting
yet again, describes the original as 'strong but primitive and naïve'. The
1934 version that MacKinnon created was based on an Austrian prayer

card of Victorian vintage which Tognieri has no hesitation in labelling as being of 'overt sentimentality'.

When he left Campbeltown in 1887, the crowds were still gazing in awe at his newly discovered work. In 1934, MacKinnon attracted crowds again. The press was there in force from all over Britain, and cinema newsreels carried the story of the elderly artist making his own pilgrimage back to Davaar. Wearing his good suit, he climbed ladders to create his third version of the Christ crucified. This time, he had no worries about using school paints: the town council paid his expenses from the Common Good Fund.

According to Hamish Mckinven's account in the *Scots Magazine* of April 1988, the inaugural ceremony to unveil the completion of this interpretation seems to have been a very different affair to the solitary and secret exit MacKinnon made after his first painting was finished. This time all the town worthies were there, including – perhaps unusually

Art teacher Ronald Tognieri has repainted the figure twice – once in 2006 in the wake of a graffiti attack. *Maureen Bell.*

for the 1930s – the Moderator of the Kintyre Presbytery and the local Catholic priest side by side. The ceremony took place on 6 June, and on 15 May of the following year Archibald MacKinnon died at his home in Nantwich at the age of eighty-five.

It became something of a tradition for the head of the art department at Campbeltown High School to restore the painting after MacKinnon's death. In the 1950s, it was John McInally who did the work. He found the painting greatly deteriorated because of water pouring into the cave. In the 1960s, John McKinnon Crawford painted a more classic, Velasquez-style figure, correcting what Tognieri refers to as 'the short stumpy arms' of the Christ figure.

Mr Tognieri did yet another restoration job in the 1970s, paid for by the community council. It remained undamaged until 2006 when a vandal, filmed on CCTV buying spray paint but never caught, 'tagged' a stencil of the revolutionary Che Guevara over the face of Christ. Tognieri was called in again and now he hopes that the painting, sealed with modern solutions, will last for another decade or two. He had more than the Che Guevara image to clean up when he got to the cave. Inside he found what he describes as 'little votive offerings', ranging from tea lights and teddy bears to poems and plastic trash. He dates such offerings to 1997 and the death of Princess Diana, which turned the old Celtic custom of leaving a stone into an unstoppable need to mark a presence with increasingly personal mementoes. Tognieri says, 'I don't feel anyone should leave anything but their thoughts in a place like this.'

The painting, changed though it is, still holds the same pull as it did when it was discovered in August 1887. Every low tide, people from all over the world can be seen making their way across the shingle causeway, known as the Dhorlin, to Davaar. A fund which was started after the vandalism may pay for an interpretation board at the pier in Campbeltown, but people like Ronald Tognieri have reservations about anything more formal or more concrete. 'It's a bit of a spreckle across the rocks and scree,' he says, 'and I think it should stay like that.' It is no longer possible to hire boats to go over to the island as they did in that first feeding frenzy over the painting: there has been a change in safety regulations. And surely the natural barrier placed by the sea between the viewer and the painting is what adds to its mystique. Whether people come because of the spirituality the painting in the cave creates, or simply because it is one of Argyll's curiosities, they come without the aid of nationwide publicity campaigns like those of the early 1900s which urged tourists to come to Campbeltown to catch the Atlantic Express – the toy town train which ran to Machrihanish on the west coast of Kintyre. After the vandalism incident, Ronald Tognieri isn't keen to spread the word. Although he admits that the image has little physical connection to the first painting, Tognieri believes there is a strong spiritual link back to the 1887 work. He says of the original, 'It was a brilliant stroke of creativity. By painting it on the wall of a sea cave which looks over to St Kieran's cave he created a spiritual connection back to the saint.' It is typical of Argyll that the curiosities of the present lead us to the past, while those of the past crowd into the present seeking our attention.

11

AN ELEGANT RELIEF

The island of Bute fails by yards to be yet another of Argyll's peninsulas and instead is an island locked in the arms of Cowal. The Kyles of Bute, those narrow stretches of water separating Bute from the mainland, are where the 9th Earl of Argyll played cat and mouse with government forces during his abortive attempt to install William of Orange on the throne in 1685, and they have been the scene of bloody battles since man put to sea. Coracles, Viking longships, royal birlinns and English warships sailed into the Kyles of Bute – and sometimes left in tatters.

Mainland Argyll boasted many royal castles where kings – and once Mary, Queen of Scots – made their presence felt when the clans on this western fringe became too fractious. Bute, however, regarded itself as somewhat superior, because it was not simply a staging post for kings trying to keep a country in order: it spawned the House of Stuart. Rothesay Castle was built by a hereditary high steward of Scotland, which office gave us the name Stewart or Stuart; the princes and kings who ruled Scotland from 1371 to 1603 and then England as well, until James VII and II was removed from the throne in 1688 – and who tried twice in the eighteenth century to reclaim the throne – were descended from that line.

The ruins of that dynasty's first fortified home are curious enough in themselves, being the remains of the only circular castle in Scotland. Rothesay Castle was attacked by the Vikings and provided a grandstand view of the Norsemen's last stand in mainland Scotland at the Battle of Largs in 1263. Before the family could draw breath, the English captured the castle in 1311 as they hounded Robert Bruce around Argyll, but as the Bruce's star went into ascendancy, so too did Rothesay Castle's fortunes and he re-took it, along with Tarbert on Loch Fyne and the other royal strongholds. The castle was partially destroyed by Cromwell's men in the British Civil Wars but it was our friend the 9th Earl of Argyll who sacked it in his last frenzied strategies to salvage his revolutionary attempts in 1685.

The ss *Columba* brought some of the many thousands of visitors to
Rothesay in the nineteenth century. *Argyll and Bute Library Service.*

This was not, of course, the end of the Stuarts of Bute. Under the 2nd
Earl of Bute, the family headquarters were moved away from Rothesay
in 1716 some seven miles to the south to a new house fit for a new
peaceful age. Mount Stuart House was built on a 300-acre estate and
was a fine home for a family with such a heritage. But in 1877 part of
the building was destroyed by fire, and out of the ashes came the 3rd
Marquess's inspired Gothic mansion, begun in 1879 and said to be one
of the most magnificent of its kind in the world.

With such a history, it is not surprising that when the Clyde coastal
towns became popular with the advent of the steamboats from the earliest years of the nineteenth century, Bute saw itself as a particularly special
resort. 'The Madeira of the Clyde' was its sobriquet and with its palm
trees and pavilions it attracted the rich and the famous to its shores. The
actor Edmund Kean must have been one of the first of the celebrities to
seek a quiet corner of the island in which to hide from their public when
he built Woodend House on a 20-acre site on the shores of Loch Fad in
1824, just twelve years after the *Comet* had made her maiden voyage and
changed the face of the Clyde forever.

Not content with the beauty nature had bestowed on Bute, man set
about enhancing it. Magnus Barefoot, Robert Bruce, Cromwell and the

9th Earl of Argyll would all be very confused were they to sail into the Kyles of Bute today and head for the old castle. Once, it guarded the shoreline; today an expanse of reclaimed land sits between it and the Firth of Clyde. In the cellars of shops built on Rothesay's Wester Road and down into Guilford Square, the former harbour wall is visible, complete with iron rings to tie up the boats. It was on this reclaimed land that the Victorians built their holiday homes, their tenements to rent out to the seasonal visitors, their entertainment palaces – and their toilets.

It is the Victorian lavatory on the modern ferry pier which is Bute's curious jewel in the crown, the last survivor of its kind in Scotland, if not the UK. This tiled edifice with its magnificent marble, copper, glass and porcelain fitments has offered elegant relief to tourists from all round the world. A urinal graced by HRH Prince Charles, Duke of Rothesay, is honoured by a plaque bearing his coat of arms, and the visitors' book contains the signatures of day-trippers and film directors, yachtsmen and pop singers, commuters and soap-opera stars.

Until it was renovated in 1994, the building was a convenience for gentlemen only. Built in 1899 at the behest of the Rothesay Harbour Trust, it was a statement of the island's quite justified self-importance.

The trust's role was to collect the harbour dues on behalf of the local community. The house at Mount Stuart was not long completed

Land was reclaimed to turn Rothesay into the capital of the Madeira of the Clyde. *Argyll and Bute Library Service.*

A cross between a botanical garden and an ornate Mediterranean
café, the Victorian lavatory is the last of its kind.

and house-guests came and went regularly. Wealthy private yachtsmen
called in at the harbour and the most famous artistes of the day were
booked to play in the theatres. The trust decided that they were to have
the best of facilities, and the hoi polloi who came on day-trips or to
spend a works holiday in a 'single end' benefited from this civic preen-
ing. Entering the lavatory is like going into a hybrid of botanic garden
and ornate Mediterranean café. It is light and airy; the walls gleam with
ceramic tiles and the ceramic mosaic floor reflects daylight from glass

ceiling panels. The three cisterns high on the walls in the main part of the lavatory are glass-sided and decorated with imitation dark-green St Anne's marble. Highly polished copper pipes feed water from the tanks down to fourteen urinals, which line two walls. Each urinal, pristine white and topped by the St Anne's marble, bears the name Twyfords Ltd, Cliffe Vale Potteries, Hanley. In the centre of the room stands an edifice more Roman fountain than basic function. Plants trail from an urn which sits on top of a marble column that serves to lift the eye from six more urinals ranged around its base. On a third wall are nine cubicles with lavatory pans made, like all the fitments here, by Twyfords in 1899 in Glasgow at a total cost of £530.

Brian Balmain is chairman of Bute Victoriana Ltd, the community business with charitable status which manages Rothesay's curious survivor from the glittering era of Clyde-coast prosperity. He says the loo was so special because Butemen saw themselves as 'a cut above the others who must have the best'. The lavatory, he says, was part of the special welcome which Rothesay offered its visitors.

Thomas William Twyford provided the 1890 fixtures and fittings for the palatial gents' lavatory on Rothesay pier.

The pale tiled exterior of the lavatory gleams to the right of the
bandstand dome, a curious landmark on the Bute coastline. *Argyll
and Bute Library Service.*

Although the first public toilets for women were available in London
in the middle of the nineteenth century, and public parks offered such
facilities around the country, the 1899 lavatory on Rothesay harbour was
for men only. Facilities for women were available in the pier buildings
– which were destroyed by fire – but they couldn't match the ornateness
of the 'gents only' palace. Not that the ladies would have been aware
of what they were excluded from: the outside of the harbour lavatory
is plain by comparison, although today it seems quite showy with its
glazed bricks of different colours arranged in patterns. No clues lie in
the outward appearance to the peacock display offset by masculine dark
woodwork which is to be found on the inside.

Twyfords, a company which had been in existence since the very decade when the 9th Earl of Argyll was burning down Rothesay Castle and
trying to escape the government ships in the Kyles of Bute, was commissioned to produce the urinals and toilets for this little palace on the
harbour. The fireclay products were among the first of a new technique
used by Thomas William Twyford in the 1890s and bear the 'Adamant'
trademark. But although these adamantine products stood the test of time,
the rest of the building fell into disrepair as Rothesay's fortunes waned
in the second half of the twentieth century. The technology which had
created the 'Madeira of the Clyde' gave way to cheap air flights; fewer

and fewer people took their 'Fair' holiday at the Clyde resort and more and more went off to gain the kind of superficial knowledge of foreign parts described by Martin Martin in his 'Curiosities of the Western Isles' preface. With a greatly reduced income, the island was in no position to maintain its curiously elaborate lavatories.

It was then that Strathclyde Building Preservation Trust stepped in to save the building and its interior. Grants of almost £300,000 were found in the early 1990s, and, by 1994, not only were the original gents' toilets restored to their former glory, but a storeroom had been converted into a ladies' lavatory. A disabled access toilet and showers were also added. The honour of opening the restored building fell to Lucinda Lambton, author of a history of lavatories, who described Rothesay's urinals as 'the most beautiful in the world'. The curiosity value of visiting a lavatory which not only provides a splendid service but is also aesthetically pleasing and historically unique means that pleasure craft make a point of stopping off in Rothesay so that passengers can use the facilities and sign the visitors' book. The restoration of the Victorian lavatory has contributed to the improved fortunes of Bute.

12

PERFIDIOUS KINTYRE

It was around 6 o'clock in the evening on 2 June 1994 when RAF Chinook helicopter ZD576 crashed on the Mull of Kintyre. The helicopter had been carrying most of the UK's senior intelligence experts on Northern Ireland and they, plus a crew of four, were all killed – a total of twenty-nine dead. It was a tragedy in human terms and a disaster politically. So many lives wasted; so much ground lost in the delicate quest to bring peace to Northern Ireland. The helicopter flew into a hillside in dense fog – far from the first time that these hills had claimed the lives of airmen, and far from the first time that the formidable Mull of Kintyre had proved to be more than a match for whatever sophisticated scientific implements and modes of transport man could devise.

The Chinook was a fairly complex piece of machinery, although in the subsequent inquiries it was suggested that unreliability of engine power and false warnings had been experienced in similar helicopters. It first hit the Mull 810 feet above sea level, about 1,500 feet east of the lighthouse. Much of the fuselage continued to travel, however, and broke up about 600 feet further north. The members of the Ulster Constabulary, MI5, and the British Army who had set out from Belfast for a conference in Inverness would have died on impact with the ground, when fire broke out. The noise of the crash was heard, but no one saw the incident because fog had reduced visibility to a few yards. For many of the local people it was no surprise to learn of the crash.

In the years that followed, inquiry after inquiry came up with unsatisfactory conclusions about the cause of the crash. The possibility that the IRA had the capability to shoot the Chinook down was considered. The mechanical state of the Chinook following a refit was discussed by experts. When the first official inquiry concluded that the crash was caused by pilot error, it wasn't only the families and friends of the airmen who were angered: the people of Kintyre questioned the decision too. The RAF board of inquiry's decision in 1995 that the two pilots were guilty of gross negligence was seen as highly unfair. The question of blame was left open at a fatal accident inquiry – the Scottish equivalent of an inquest – in 1996, and in 2000 the House of Commons Defence Committee report and a Commons Public Accounts Committee also left the question of blame open or challenged the original conclusion. The taint of blame, however, still lay heavily on the names of the dead pilots, Flight Lieutenant Jonathan Tapper and Flight Lieutenant Rick Cook. A further inquiry took place in the House of Lords in 2001, and when its findings were published in January 2002, the verdicts of gross negligence by the pilots were declared unjustified.

This brought a sigh of relief in Kintyre. So many young men had died on the Kintyre hills; so many mariners had died off the formidable Mull. 'Gross negligence' was surely not the cause of all those fatalities.

If the Cairn na Burgh islands are the Rosslyn Chapel of Argyll, hiding not the Holy Grail but the treasures of the Classical world, then the Mull of Kintyre must be Argyll's Bermuda Triangle. The high, steep cliffs of the Mull presented a formidable threat to the mariners of the past. In the twentieth century, airmen grew to dread approaching the tip of the Kintyre peninsula. During the Second World War, the hillsides became littered with the wreckage of planes.

And the accidents haven't stopped. In May 2006, the Machrihanish air ambulance crashed just after midnight as it travelled from Glasgow to the Mull of Kintyre to pick up a sick child. The pilot and paramedic died and the wreckage was found in the sea some 8 miles from Campbeltown airport. This time there was no fog; indeed, the coastguard reported that the weather conditions were reasonable and that he could not speculate on the cause of the accident. The twin-engined plane was said to have lined up in the correct way to approach the airport, but then it disappeared off the radar screen and the alarm was raised by the air traffic controller.

There are, of course, many theories about the tragedies which have happened on and around the Mull of Kintyre. One has been fuelled by the RAF base at Machrihanish, where all sorts of futuristic operations have been said to take place. Golfers are said to have witnessed a 'V' shape with a vague shimmering space above it rushing across the calm sea. They heard loud roaring above their heads which seemed to come from over the RAF-NATO air strip. This is accepted by the conspiracy theorists as evidence of a 'cloaking device' which renders ships, aircraft or airfields invisible. While this may be strategically helpful, it could also, the theory goes, play havoc with computerised instruments on other aircraft or ships in the vicinity. Others suggest that futuristic planes have been tested from Machrihanish.

These theories do not explain the crashes which took place before such experimentation, nor those that have occurred since the former RAF houses were sold off to all comers, who might well notice such strange goings-on, and the base mothballed. The blame might as well be placed firmly at the feet of the standing stones, with a claim of druidic energy forces pulling aircraft off course. The Mull has two chambered cairns in its centre, two to the south-east, eight cairns, a barrow and standing stones. Moving up Kintyre, there is one chambered cairn at Blast Hill and another at Gort na h-Ulaidhe in Glen Lussa on the east coast, north of Campbeltown. There are cairns at Corriechrevie and Machrihanish – why not blame the ley lines said to stretch out their magnetic forces between such cairns for this curious phenomenon? Local people remain more concerned about those who have lost their lives than with all of the fanciful theories.

Jenny Mitchell – now Campbell – was just nine years old at the out-break of World War II. She lived with her parents, Neil and Jennie, and two brothers at Killeonan, a mile and a half from Stewarton, the little township on the way to the Mull, and her father was the gardener at Kilchreist Castle. At that time, the airport was at Straths Farm, a mile or so from Stewarton, and the Fleet Air Arm was stationed there. This older airfield predated the war and had been used by ambulance planes before the Fleet Air Arm took over. The latter also commandeered Kilchreist Castle, where the Mitchells got to know their squadron leader, a son of the Earl of Glasgow. Schools and hotels were commandeered by the armed forces. Kintyre swarmed with troops. Mr Mitchell continued to grow vegetables at the castle to help feed those billeted there, but he also eked out the family income by making wreaths for Mr Wallace, the un-dertaker, in Campbeltown. Jenny remembers that this was the way that she and her brothers knew that a plane had crashed, from the under-taker's solemn visit to their father to ask for wreaths. They were simple affairs, the flowers of the season. Snowdrops, lilac, monbretia were all brought into sad service to commemorate the lives of these young men who died so far from home. Jenny said, 'There were an awful lot of them and it often seemed to be when the snowdrops were out. A few of the

The modern road to the Mull of Kintyre lighthouse is single track
and tortuous. This stretch leads towards the Gap.

old shepherds said it was the currents that were drawing the planes into
the hill. In these days the hills were full of sheep and they would see the
flights of the birds of prey.'

The Mull was difficult, not only for planes, but for boats. It is said
that the Corryvreckan whirlpool between Jura and Scarba offers the most
dangerous waters to fishermen. Whether its boiling waters are due to a
meeting of currents and tides or a Pictish chieftain angrily complaining
about losing his life there and having to live beneath the waves, there
is no denying its perils. The Mull of Kintyre is also an area where seas
meet; in addition there are thick mists and high winds. It is the reason
the Crinan Canal was built – not only to save miles and time but to save
lives. Every time one of the little Loch Fyne fishing boats rounded the
Mull it was at risk.

There is little that is welcoming about the Mull, although there is no
denying its fearsome majesty which rears up so suddenly from the lush
pastures around Carskiey. The road to the lighthouse is single track and
formidable. It narrows, twists around rocky outcrops, climbs up to 700
feet and then on to the Gap, which sits 1,350 feet above sea-level. There
is a neat car park here and a turning place for cars – because no vehicles
are allowed beyond that point. Few would want to flout that ruling and

attempt what the Argyll writer Alasdair Carmichael called 'two fearsome hairpin bends round sheer cliffs' after he had visited the Mull in 1970 for *The Scots Magazine*; the road beyond the Gap has not improved since. A long-outdated signboard, erected by Strathclyde Council in the days of regionalisation, lies on the ground: it once gave information about the kind of vehicles allowed to park here. The neat depiction of a caravan bears a red cross. Any driver who manages to manoeuvre a caravan as far as the Gap deserves a medal and would probably need an overnight stop to allow his knees to stop shaking. Another wooden noticeboard reminds visitors that in the hills around them lies the wreckage of aircraft, and a cairn has been built on the site of the 1994 crash in memory of the Chinook victims.

Two centuries before, it was the frequency of shipwrecks which made a lighthouse on the Mull a necessity. Around 1790, the Duke of Argyll had cleared the Mull for a sheep-walk and only a couple of houses

Cairn erected in memory of those who died in the Chinook helicopter tragedy of 1994. *Muriel and Jim Adam, Edinburgh.*

Mull of Kintyre lighthouse, built by Thomas Smith and his stepson
Robert Stevenson at the end of the 1780s. Stonemasons found the
site 'difficult to access and so remote'.

remained, occupied by shepherds. Previously, a crofter-shepherd living
near the site of today's lighthouse had kept a light in his window as a
guide to mariners. There were still few official lighthouses, but in 1785
the Collector of Customs in Campbeltown had been asked to estimate
the costs of building and operating a lighthouse on the Mull of Kintyre.
The collector had replied on 1 March 1786, 'We beg leave to observe
that a lighthouse on the Mull of Kintyre would certainly be of the greatest advantage to navigation', adding that ships from America and the
West Indies frequently made mistakes travelling between the Irish coast
and the Mull. He had no expertise to estimate costs but stressed that a
light on the top of the Mull would be 'covered with fog and clouds'.

Things moved apace. In August that year a meeting of commissioners for erecting lighthouses had approved one on the Mull, and, early in
1787, the Duke of Argyll, his chamberlain and the Provost of Campbeltown had all responded positively to requests for a lease on two acres
of ground for the new lighthouse, keeper's cottage and garden. Thomas
Smith was appointed as the first engineer and received instruction from
Ezekiel Walker – at a cost to the Board of Commissioners of 50 guineas

– who had built the light at Lyme Regis in England. This Thomas Smith had in 1786 become the stepfather of a fourteen-year-old named Robert Stevenson. Robert would succeed his stepfather as the Northern Lighthouse Board's chief engineer in 1796, and perhaps the fifty guineas were well spent. Thomas and Robert became the founding members of the family known today as 'the lighthouse Stevensons', with four generations building innovative lighthouses in the most dangerous waters of Scotland, from Bell Rock in the east, round to Ardnamurchan Point and Skerryvore off Tiree in the west.

The Duke of Argyll charged 5 shillings a year for the 2-acre site. He also insisted it be enclosed and that the keeper did not have a dog, as this would be a danger to stock on his sheep-walk. Not quite such a danger, it seems, as the wild cats which prowled the area and threatened both sheep and keeper's safety. And not quite such an inconvenience as the sheep eating the keeper's vegetables – he could hardly pop to the shop to buy more. This clause in the contract was hotly disputed in later years. Meanwhile, the board was finding it difficult to get builders for 'a place so difficult to access and so remote'. Three stonemasons were then sent from Edinburgh to do the work. The charge hand, George Shields, was paid 4 shillings and 2 pence a day and his assistants, John and William Purdie, received 3 shillings a day. The stores and materials were landed 6 miles away and transported on horseback in loads of a hundredweight per animal. No animal was allowed to do more than one journey a day, an interesting nod towards animal welfare at a time when men's safety and conditions were rarely considered. It was 16 miles to Campbeltown and the last 5 were over a mountain without a track. When the son of the first keeper died, an obituary noted the difficulties of aiming for a gap in the mountain – now 'the Gap' on maps – to reach the lighthouse. The lighthouse was finished in three months despite the difficulties, and the light was hung on 6 March 1788 by Thomas Smith. Smith – with a care that was typical of him, and of the Stevenson engineers who followed him in the family firm – showed great concern for the welfare of the keepers. He was doubtful that the keeper would be able to grow anything on this desolate spot, and he insisted that peats be laid in before the keeper took up his position. William Harvey, a former ship's master, was the first keeper and Smith fought his corner when the Duke of Argyll's company made life difficult for him. 'They seem to treat the man as if he were a thief or a sheep-stealer and insist upon it that they have a right to prevent him from keeping a dog or a gun by the agreement with the Duke of Argyll', he reported. He recommended that Harvey have both gun and dog, saying, 'If he cannot be trusted with these he surely ought not to have such an important trust as the lighthouse.'

By 1820, Robert Stevenson was a man of some importance in the lighthouse world and had invented intermittent and flashing lights. He came back to the Mull lighthouse, where as a teenager he had assisted his new stepfather, and carried out some modernisation. His journey would have been as difficult as those undertaken by George Shields and the Purdies when they built the light, and his stepfather when he put in the first lantern. It was not until the 1830s that the commissioners built a 4 foot 3 inch-wide bridle track from Glemanuilt, a farm at the start of the arduous climb to the lighthouse. In 1848, McNeill of Carskiey granted the commissioners a right of access to Glemanuilt and a proper road was built. The light was electrified in 1976 and automated in 1996. Small craft, fishing boats and puffers all learned to seek safety under the cliffs of the lighthouse.

There is no denying that this is a beautiful place, but one where nature is in control. In the days of the bridle path, a successor to William Harvey, the first light-keeper, faced a tragedy as keen as any experienced since on the Mull. His children became ill one winter when deep snow had fallen. There was no chance of the doctor being able to reach the light and all four children died. The keeper and his wife tried to take the little bodies on a pony sled to Southend for burial but this proved impossible, so the children were buried on the hill at a dizzying height above the sea. They no longer rest alone up there: sadly, too many twentieth-century air crews have joined them in this bleak place.

From here to Ireland is just 12 miles – the distance one Victorian engineer wanted to cover with a causeway and another with a tunnel under the sea. On a clear day, it seems that you can you can reach out and touch the Irish coast. On a bad day – and the swiftness of change here can turn good to bad in minutes – you can't see a hand in front of you and the solid mass of the Mull is ready to swallow all comers. It is alarming enough with your feet on the ground, but unimaginably terrifying with nothing between you and heather-clad rock or peat bog but the flimsy shell of a small aircraft. And how small and helpless the seamen must feel out there on the water as the mist muffles them in a threatening silence – except for the distant roar of the sea as it pounds with the ferocity of the Old Woman of the Thunderbolt against the precipitous cliffs.

Even the miracle of the Stevenson lighthouse that replaced the brave little light which shone from 1788 cannot help mariner or airman when the weather changes for the worse around the Mull of Kintyre.

In recent years, patient detective work was carried out by Duncan McArthur of Peninver, with help from Bobby Duncan, Alistair MacKinley and Chris Blair, in order to compile a database of the twenty-two World War II planes which crashed between Tarbert, Loch Fyne and the Mull of Kintyre, along with those which have fallen foul of the Mull in peacetime – at least the same number again. Duncan, who could see the Mull from his house on the other side of the peninsula – usually swathed in a cap of mist whatever the weather – also sought the help of RAF Atlantic House, RAF Machrihanish and the Civil Aviation Authority at Atlantic House. He called in help from Campbeltown Registry Office and from the researcher Alan Leishman of Ardrossan in his efforts to locate crash sites, identify the dead and make contact with bereaved families.

Planes lost in the early war years, such as an Anson which went down in October 1943 near Strone farm in Southend parish, were often not discovered for decades. Wreckage was found near the site of the Anson crash as recently as 2005. A Beaufort crashed above the Gap on the Mull on 2 September 1942, killing the crew instantly. Much of its remains have been found since Duncan started his quest. Duncan also located the wreckage of a Vickers Wellington LB 137 which went down on 1 December 1943 after taking off from RAF Silloth on the Solway Firth on a training mission for the ongoing battle against Germany. The plane was flown by a crew of six and was armed with 7.7 millimetre machine-guns. It was able to cruise at just over 400 kilometres an hour and it was carrying 2,014 kilograms of bombs. The plane crashed on the western slope of Beinn na Lice on the Mull and all of the crew were killed. The two pilots were taken home to England for burial – Jeffrey Duddridge, twenty-six, in Sheffield, and Harry Fransfield, just twenty-one years old, in Somerset. Neil Mitchell would have made wreaths for the others: navigator Charles Cooper, twenty-five; Victor Francis Sutter, twenty-five, who was an air gunner; Flight Sergeants Reginald Canavan, twenty-five; and Robert Wardrop. The four were buried in Kilkerran cemetery, and the wreckage of their plane – the twin-engined mainstay of

Neil Mitchell made the wreaths for young Reg Canavan and his
friend Vic Sutter, who were among those who died when a Vickers-
Wellington crashed on the Mull in 1943. *Duncan McArthur.*

the air fleet in World War II – was in part salvaged by the RAF. However,
a local scrap dealer illegally moved some of the remains back to the little car park at the Gap, and after he was warned off by the police the
RAF officials recorded the car park as the official crash site. It was only
in 2006 that the true site of the crash was discovered, during a search
for the whereabouts of a Neptune aircraft which had gone down on the
Mull in 1956. Pathetic remnants of twisted and rusted metal with partly
obscured serial numbers are often all that remains to mark where men
have met their deaths.

A number of Hudsons are on Duncan's list. These were part of a con-
signment of planes brought to the UK across the Atlantic. They had first
been sent on ships, but after a hundred were lost in a U-boat attack, it
was decided to fly them to Britain using young pilots from the Canadian
Royal Airforce. The twelve planes which set off from Gander in Canada
for St Eval in England were small and their fuel capacity was limited.
The pilots were told to head first for Prestwick on the Ayrshire coast,
but to make for Northern Ireland if their fuel gauge was reading low.

On 25 July 1941, Flight Lieutenant Fergus Keith Arnold of the Royal Canadian Air Force saw that he didn't have enough fuel to get to Prestwick. He tried instead to fly into Limavady but went off course. The Hudson crashed just below a cottage at Feorlin on the Mull road. The thirty-year-old was killed instantly, along with Wilfred Bratherton, his radio operator, and Flight Sergeant Percy Keast. Percy and Wilfred were both just twenty-one years old. Ten of the other eleven Hudsons made it to Prestwick but one, flown by a former Hollywood stunt pilot named Captain Bob Perlick, had to land in Northern Ireland.

Wilfred Bratherton's passport. He died on 25 July 1941 when his
Hudson crashed at Feorlin on the Mull of Kintyre road.
Duncan McArthur.

Much of the debris which is found is a jumble of heat-contorted metal, but, as a reminder of the human tragedy, Duncan McArthur and his team of dedicated researchers recently found a watch inscribed with Fergus Keith Arnold's name.

One of the crashes which happened in peacetime involved an aircraft from HMS *Dido*, which was escorting the Royal Yacht. The Wasp crashed at around 10 o'clock on the night of 12 August 1970, when the visibility was low and rain was driving across the Mull. The site of the accident was close to that of a Beaufighter's demise in 1943. Both crewmen, Lt. Com. RNAF D.M. Carr and Lt RNAF T. Blakely, were reported dead, but although one crewman was killed at the site, the other was found the next day wandering dazed on the hillside. When the rescue teams go out to search for missing aircrew, their task is akin to seeking the proverbial needle in a haystack. Many of the sites are dangerous to reach. Many are in peat bogs. Some are by innocuously pretty streams near picturesque farmhouses.

The youth of the dead wartime crews adds to the poignancy of these crashes, but, as a poem discovered by Duncan McArthur indicates, these young men had enviable experiences behind them even though they were often cut down at the start of their twenties. This was written for his parents by Pilot Officer John Gillespie Magee of No. 412 Squadron, Royal Canadian Airforce. He was a Spitfire pilot who died at the age of nineteen in 1941:

High Flight

Oh! I have slipped the surly bonds of earth
And danced the skies on laughter-silvered wings.
Sunward I've climbed, and joined the tumbling mirth
Of sun-split clouds – and done a hundred things
You have not dreamed of – wheeled and soared and swung
High in the sunlit silence. Hov'ring there
I've chased the shouting wind along, and flung
My eager craft through footless halls of air . . .
Up the long delirious burning blue,
I've topped the windswept heights with easy grace
Where never lark, or even eagle flew –
And while with silent, lifting mind I trod
The high untrespassed sanctity of space,
Put out my hand and touched the face of God.

The blame for the numerous tragedies has often been placed on a sometimes inexplicable loss of communication, but this is at odds with another curious fact about this southern part of Kintyre: Machrihanish, on the coast to the north of the Mull, was chosen as the site for the first radio transmission across the Atlantic – and that transmission was a success. In January 1906, radio contact was made between Brant Rock in America and Machrihanish in Scotland by the Canadian-born inventor Reginald A. Fessenden. A 420-foot-high transmission tower was built by the National Electric Signalling Company in America, and on 2 January 1906 Morse signals started to go out to a tower in Machrihanish. It took some fine tuning, but on 8 January a response finally came back: 'Condensers working very satisfactorily.' These were the first words to be transmitted from this side of the Atlantic to the American continent. By the autumn of that year, it wasn't only the dots and dashes of Morse code that were crossing the sea: the first-ever radio programme was broadcast from the American mast on Christmas Eve 1906 and the voices were picked up by Machrihanish.

It was Marconi, however, who walked off with the Nobel Prize for Physics in 1909, despite having broadcast across the Atlantic just one way. Fessenden and Machrihanish had been instrumental in paving the

Reginald A. Fessenden transmitted from the other side of the Atlantic to Machrihanish in 1906. Not all signals are scrambled by the mass of the Mull. *Duncan McArthur.*

Reg Canavan's war grave at Kilkerran cemetery in Cambeltown. A poignant reminder of all who have lost their lives on the Mull, one of the worst air-accident sites in Britain. *Muriel and Jim Adam, Edinburgh.*

way for modern radio by developing a method of using continuous radio waves that could carry voices and music as well as codes. Marconi's first transmission used a 'spark gap transmitter' which did not carry voices easily. Today, neither the Machrihanish nor the Brant Rock transmitters have survived, but at least Kintyre remembered to commemorate the centenary of that special day when Fessenden made real radio history.

Sadly, that first successful broadcast was no lucky talisman. As the twentieth century progressed, the curious forces which play around the Mull of Kintyre, whatever their source may be, conspired to take many lives. Duncan McArthur, who sadly died before this book went to print, was under no illusion that anything other than pilot error in Mull of Kintyre's notoriously bad weather is responsible for the grim database he was building. That a Neptune, an Armstrong Whitworth Whitley, a Wellington and a Chinook should have gone down within a sixth of a mile of each other is something he found unutterably sad, but a fact of Kintyre life. Arthur Helsby, who took part in a rescue effort after a Neptune with a crew of nine came down on the west slope of Beinn na Lice at about 1,300 feet in 1956, has learnt that 'freak meteorological conditions' confronted the pilots of both the Chinook helicopter in 1994 and the Neptune in 1956. On the Mull, for 'freak' one has all too often to read 'normal'. Over a hundred and twenty lives have been lost around the Mull, making it one of the worst sites in Britain for air accidents.

Those for whom the snowdrop and lilac wreaths were made by Neil Mitchell during the war are buried in Kilkerran graveyard, each with a military headstone like Reg Canavan's – his erected by the Australian Air Force. There is also a formal memorial for the servicemen at Kilkerran which contrasts poignantly with the traditional cairn on the hillside for the Chinook's dead and the markers on the four little graves of children whose deaths could not even be commemorated by a posy of snow-drops. The wartime airmen were lost in number: each plane carried up to eight of a crew. They were strangers to the young Jenny Mitchell, now Mrs Campbell, but their deaths affected her deeply. 'They weren't shot down,' she said. 'They hit the hill. They didn't die because of the war but because of Kintyre.'

BIBLIOGRAPHY

Argyll Inventory of Monuments, Volumes 1, 2, 3, 4, 20. *Royal Commission on the Ancient and Historical Monuments of Scotland.* Edinburgh

Argyllshire Advertiser

Argyllshire Herald

Baillie, Lady G., *The Household Book of Lady Grisell Baillie.* Reprint: Scottish History Society, 1911

Barton, J., *The Proposed Tunnel between Scotland and Ireland, International Engineering Congress, Glasgow 1901.* Clowes and Son, 1902

Buchan, J.W., *A History of Peeblesshire.* Jackson Wyle, 1925–7

Campbell, H., *Abstracts of the General Register of Sasines of Argyll, Bute and Dunbarton, otherwise known as the Argyll Sasines.* W. Brown, 1934

Gillies, P. H., *Netherlorn and Its Neighbourhood.*1909

The Glynns: *Journal of the Glens of Antrim Historical Society,* Volume 19. Antrim Historical Society,1991

Grant, W., *Tweeddale.* Oliver and Boyd, 1948

Galbraith, D.O. and Longbottom, D., *A History of Muckairn Parish,* Muckairn Parish Church

Irish Builder

Kilbrandon and Kilchattan Census for Belnahua. HMSO, 1861

Macassey, L. L. and Scott, W., *Report on the Proposed Railway Tunnel between Scotland and Ireland.* Harrison and Sons, and C. Aitchison, 1885

MacDonald, The Rev. C., Priest of Moidart. *Moidart: Among the Clanranalds,* 1889. Reprint: Birlinn, 1996

MacMillan, N. S. C., *The Campbeltown and Machrihanish Light Railway.* Plateway Press, 1993

MacNab, P., *Mull and Iona Highways and Byways.* Luath Guides, 1986

Martin, M, *Curiosities of Art and Nature,* 1703. New edition by the Islands Book Trust, 2003

McAlpine, Sir Robert and Sons Ltd., *Fifth Monthly Report, 1868–1919*

McLynn, F., *Charles Edward Stewart*. Oxford University Press, 1991

Minutes of the General Assembly of the Church of Scotland, 1883. Church of Scotland, 1883

Murray, K.W., *Murray Pedigrees*. www.murrayof stanhope.com

Neilson, R., *Second Report to the Commissioners and Trustees for Improving Fisheries and Manufactures in Scotland*. 1755

Oban Times

Shedden, H.,'The Story of Lorne, its Islands and Oban' in *Oban Times*, 1938

The Statistical Accounts of Argyll, HMSO, 1792 and 1845

Swire, O., *The Inner Hebrides and Their Legends*. Collins, 1964

Withall, M., *Easdale, Belnahua, Luing and Seil: The Islands that Roofed the World*, Luath, 1981

Yuill, J. and I. Young, 'Hide-outs in the hills – Paper Cave, Argyll' in *Grampian Speleological Group Bulletin*, January 1980

INDEX